KU-166-927

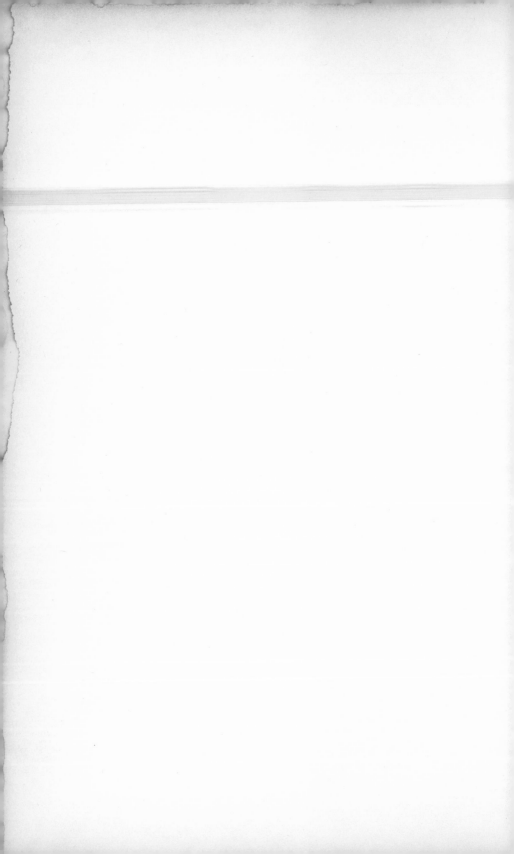

A Conservatory Manual

A Conservatory Manual

Deenagh Goold-Adams

CENTURY

LONDON MELBOURNE AUCKLAND JOHANNESBURG

Copyright © Deenagh Goold-Adams 1987 (text)
Copyright © Sources listed in Acknowledgements 1987
(illustrations)

Produced by Open Books Publishing Ltd, Beaumont House, Wells,
Somerset BA5 2LD

Designed by Humphrey Stone

All rights reserved

First published in 1987 by Century Hutchinson Ltd,
Brookmount House, 62–65 Chandos Place, Covent Garden,
London WC2N 4NW

Century Hutchinson Australia Pty Ltd,
PO Box 496, 16–22 Church Street, Hawthorn, Victoria 3122,
Australia

Century Hutchinson New Zealand Ltd,
PO Box 40–86, Glenfield, Auckland 10,
New Zealand

Century Hutchinson South Africa Pty Ltd,
PO Box 337, Bergvlei, 2012 South Africa

British Library Cataloguing in Publication Data

  Goold.Adams, Deenagh
    A conservatory manual. — (The Gardener's
    Library)
    1. Garden rooms   2. Indoor gardening
    I. Title   II. Series
    635'.0483   SB419
    ISBN 0–7126–1146–0 (Paperback)
    ISBN 0–7126–1752–3 (Hardback)

Set in the United Kingdom
Printed and bound in the United Kingdom

Contents

Acknowledgements

The author wishes to acknowledge the encouragement and advice she received from Anthony Huxley and much practical help from Patrick Taylor.

The author and publishers are extremely grateful for advice on plant names to Roy Cheek of Cannington College of Agriculture and Horticulture and to John Woodhams of The Royal Botanic Gardens, Kew. They would also like to thank owners of conservatories who allowed them, and their contents, to be photographed – especially Adrian and Daphne Butler, Victor Montagu, and Hugh and Muriel Tracy.

The sources for the illustrations are as follows: Amdega Limited (2–3); Roy Cheek (17–18, 20, 25, 29–30, 36, 38–41, 49, 52, 56–7, 61 and 63); Richard and Deenagh Goold-Adams (1, 5, 10–11, 19, 21, 31, 34, 37, 45–8, 51 and 53); Pam Holt (26–7, 33, 58); Patrick Taylor (4, 6–9, 12–15, 22–24, 28, 32, 35, 42–44, 51, 54–5, 59–60 and 62).

1

Introduction

A conservatory is for people. That, to me, is the essential difference between a conservatory and a greenhouse. The point of view and the life-style of the occupants is paramount. There may well be more than one person in charge and they may not agree about the image they wish to present to the world. But for the conservatory to be a success it will have to play a part in their actual lives. Both the people and the plants need to be happy.

The conservatory may be built to lead out into the garden or to blot out an undesirable outlook. It may be used for elegant entertaining or as a place to hang out washing or feed cats. It may even have to accommodate the many diverse objects for which there is no room elsewhere. Statues, prams, drawing-boards, washing machines, drums and even large dogs have found a home under glass. There is a tendency to build on a glass extension when the home will no longer contain all the activities pursued there, or when some member of the family needs to get away from the obsessive interests of the others. Obviously the plants required to complement or to mask such a variety of situations must be conjured up in the eye of the beholder! I can only hope to jog the memory and widen the choice, with perhaps, a hint of caution here and there. At the same time I recognise that an increasing number of people build on a conservatory as an extra room partly because glass is cheaper than bricks and mortar and permission to build more easily obtained.

Today every part of the home needs to have some practical purpose and we have come to expect a decorative background to most activities. In our increasingly well-lit and well-heated homes many plants have joined us which in the past could be grown only in greenhouses.

The original purpose of the earliest conservatories was to conserve through the winter tender plants that would spend the summer out of doors. Soon the idea of people being able to enjoy the plants in protected surroundings in inclement weather took over and has persisted ever since. The first fashionable heyday of the conservatory was during the fifty years from 1850 to 1900. Today's revival is once more encouraged by an expanding and affluent middle class with leisure to spend in the home and a wealth of plants to grow.

I cannot guess what part any particular conservatory is destined to play in any particular life, but the purpose of this book is to introduce the people to the plants they need to know to give substance to their individual dreams. In some ways this is like computer dating, but I hope it will be more helpful and less hazardous.

An incredible variety of structures may claim to be conservatories today in that they are glass-covered and contain plants. I aim to include them all in so far as the possible choice of plants is concerned. This covers every temperature from the totally unheated to those kept at room temperature. The questions that have to be answered are not only which plants might be grown in a given location, but also which plants will best respond to the care available, while playing an appropriate part in the chosen decorative style. Frankly, there are plants for plant haters as well as for plant lovers.

Every one of us has artistic preferences, favourite colours, sentimental associations and special interests. We also have opinions about what is suited to our own style of living. Even political views probably play their part in plant choice. If you do not believe me, just imagine a row of window boxes each planted by the leaders of our political parties! Even if they only had half a dozen plants to choose from no two window boxes would be alike. I suspect also that the results would correspond with something we would all recognize as characteristic of each personal and party viewpoint.

While conditions of light, temperature and space are often imposed on us, the choice of plants and the manner in which they are presented is entirely in our own hands. The atmosphere too can be that of a greenhouse, a draw-ingroom, an art gallery, a desert, a jungle or what you will. It is possible to have a deliberately period style to match the architecture of the house or to highlight a particular personal interest. The plants themselves may play a major or a minor role.

I do not believe that the best decorative effects are often achieved by the best gardeners. It is the seeing eye that counts. The plants do not have to be rare or costly to enhance a scene. It is the relationship of shapes, textures and colours and above all the effects of light that spell success or failure.

Some of the plants that spring to mind as 'conservatory' plants were popular in the days when there were gardeners to bring them in to be displayed at their best, and to take them away again a few days later to spend the rest of the year out of sight. Today we are unlikely to have the necesssary back-up space, inclination or time for that kind of thing. We can have temporary plants for a splash of colour and then discard them, but we need to be much more selective in our choice of the more permanent inhabitants of our conservatories. It is worth remembering that the quality of the leaves is no less important than the beauty of the flowers.

In a private conservatory there is no reasonable excuse for growing plants one does not like. The only problem should be in acquiring plants worthy of one's care and gathering enough knowledge to enable them to survive long enough to give satisfaction.

In fact I keep meeting people who are caring for plants they have not chosen and do not greatly admire. Not only that, but the people are made to feel inferior because the plants do not thrive. This is a sorry state of affairs. I will try very hard in this book to avoid making all the plants sound beautiful and virtuous and the people ignorant and incompetent! This can easily happen in gardening books. I do assure you that, if I had done the right thing at the right time by every pot plant I have ever owned, I would not only have died of heat exhaustion years ago but my plants would fill acres of glass! It is impossible to grow plants efficiently without them increasing in size and number every day. Those in whose care plants never grow larger have much to be thankful for.

The next chapter throws light on the history and development of cultivation under glass. Those who are in a hurry to build or furnish their own conservatory may wish to read this later and go straight to the following chapter.

2

The Origins of the Conservatory

The conservatory has a grand history even though the precise definition of what is and what is not a conservatory will always be debated. Horticultural developments are closely linked with the social and economic conditions of the age. Each distinct phase in our history has encouraged a different approach to the plants we grow and to the surroundings of our homes. We know that our Roman conquerors grew exotic fruit and vegetables under translucent protection made of thin sheets of mica or talc. They also had a very much better understanding of under-floor heating than is generally found today, yet our plant houses were not heated in this way for hundreds of years. The Romans received their horticultural inspiration from the east and used Syrian slaves to cultivate their gardens. Far Eastern nations had also studied the art of gardening many centuries before we took it seriously. A degree of prosperity, civilization and peace is necessary for elaborate ornamental gardening.

The Elizabethan period brought the enclosure of gardens and the beginning of the introduction of the multitude of new plants from distant lands that were to transform the landscape and also the diet of the people of Britain. The use of heated walls to force early fruit began at that time. Cherries, grapes, peaches, apricots and figs were already grown. Amazingly, Queen Elizabeth I visited the first orange garden in England in 1599.

It was in fact the orange and the French style of gardening which led to the construction of the first permanent buildings to protect tender plants. Although the first orange pip is reputed to have been grown in Britain in 1561, the use of orange trees in containers in the French manner spread from Italy through contact with the French court. At that time evergreens themselves had a rarity, as so few are native to Britain. Although so unsuitable for culture in Britain it is easy to understand the attraction of the orange with its glossy evergreen foliage, scented flowers and edible fruit.

At first, temporary wooden shelters were used to protect or 'conserve' orange trees and other tender 'greens' such as myrtle, rosemary, pomegranate and bay laurel through the winter. John Evelyn is generally credited with having introduced both the words greenhouse and conservatory into the English language in the middle of the seventeenth century. He does not appear to have felt that there was any clear distinction between them as we have come to believe. In any case the structures he had in mind had little in common with the conservatory of today. But in time the need for a better looking building to tone in with the architecture of the house led to the invention of the orangery. This was built of brick or stone with a slate roof. The walls were solid on three sides with tall windows in the south wall.

The orangery dates from the last quarter of the seventeenth century. We know that Louis XIV was already superbly equipped at Versailles by 1685. The one designed by Wren and Vanbrugh for Queen Anne at Kensington Palace in 1704 is one of the oldest still standing in Britain. The orangery is, however, mainly a feature of the eighteenth century. For a hundred years it was a frequent addition to the many fine houses that were being built all over the country. For the eighteenth century was a period when gentlemen took an interest in scientific subjects: in botany and in the 'curiosities' of the vegetable kingdom. Growing plants indoors purely for their beauty was not yet part of the pattern. The big estates, however, had a whole range of wood and glass structures used for forcing fruit. The small panes of poor quality glass still hampered the skill of the gardeners, although the manufacture of sheet glass had become possible in 1688. Glass was to remain a luxury material until the repeal of the glass tax in 1845, when it dropped to a sixth of its former cost.

It was the Dutch who pioneered the use of stoves in horticulture, and the accession to the British throne of William and Mary in 1688 brought Dutch influence and horticultural skills to our gardens. The word stove was used both for the object itself and also for the plant house it heated. Soon there were outside stoves with flues in walls or floors of lean-to greenhouses. This made it possible to grow tropical fruits. The first pineapple was grown in 1720 and the culture of pineapples came to be the test of a skilled gardener. There were still great difficulties with heating, as flues leaked poisonous fumes, and it was not yet clear to people that wheeling a trolley full of glowing charcoal through the greenhouses on cold nights was not a good idea. Heavy shutters and mats were used to keep out the cold and the solid roofs were insulated with straw, but the need for ventilation and particularly light in winter was not well understood. Fermentation beds of tan-bark and manure were used for pineapples and the most tender plants. These were said to retain their heat for six months.

Meanwhile industrialisation came earlier to Britain than to our continental neighbours. Roads were vastly improved and soon followed by canals and then railways. In a hundred years life was totally transformed. It was only at the end of the eighteenth century that iron began to be used for construction. This was essential for the creation of the larger, lighter and more elaborate forms of glasshouse of the Victorian age.

John Claudius Loudon, who was one of the greatest influences on British gardening, published his famous *Encyclopaedia of Gardening* in 1822. In the same year the water circulating boiler was invented. Four years later Loudon founded the first regular gardening journal, *The Gardener's Magazine*. He was a travelled and inventive man and built experimental glasshouses, as well as keeping a large personal collection of tender exotic plants. Some of his ideas were only later put into practice by Joseph Paxton.

We tend to think of Paxton as the creator of the great age of horticultural glass in which Britain led the world. As with most great men the timing of his birth gave him the opportunity for his well-earned success. He was born in 1801 and went to work for the Duke of Devonshire in 1826. Ten years later building started on the great conservatory at Chatsworth, which was to be the largest glass building in the country. It measured 84.5m x 37.5m (123ft x 277ft) with a height of 20m (67ft) and was finished by 1841. It was the first glass roof of ridge and furrow construction with a curved surface and stood in a garden that was world famous. Queen Victoria and the assembled company were able to drive through this fabulous conservatory in carriages on her visit in 1843. It was finally demolished in 1920.

A fascinating building that we are still able to see is the palm house at Bicton Gardens near East Budleigh in Devonshire (see *Plates 1* and *5*). These gardens were originally laid out in the grand French manner in 1735 and are open to the public during the summer. The palm house (sometimes described as a conservatory) was probably constructed by the firm of W. & D. Bailey to whom John Loudon had assigned the rights to his design for the curved wrought iron sash bar in 1818. The Bicton palm house is a relatively small domed building of iron with small panes of glass. Ventilation is by means of apertures in the solid back wall.

Ten years later the great palm house at Kew was completed. Even today more than a century later the first sight of this glorious building makes a memorable impact on the mind. If ever there was a building that visibly celebrated a triumphant period in a nation's history, this is it. The cast and wrought iron structure on a stone base was originally glazed in green glass. It is almost 110m (360ft) long and the central section is 20m (66ft) high. The floor was of cast iron grills with hot pipes below. It was originally heated by 12 coal-fired boilers that could maintain a temperature of 27°C (80°F) even in freezing weather. The smoke was taken below ground to an Italian-style campanile 130m (430ft) away to avoid spoiling the outline of the palm house with a chimney. The coal for the boilers also came in by an underground tunnel.

Those who visit the Golden Gate Park in San Francisco will find a Victorian palm house that was originally sent out round Cape Horn by sailing ship for a private client. Britain's colonial empire did much to stimulate the commercial exploitation of pre-fabricated buildings at an early stage in their history, as they could be sent out to parts of the world where there was little manufacturing capacity or skilled labour. The gold rush in California and the settlement of Australia were just two events which caused buildings made in Britain to be sent round the world. Houses, iron bridges, warehouses and even lighthouses were exported in pieces to be assembled on the spot.

By the middle of the nineteenth century we were ready for the full flowering of horticultural glass. Although there was still a lively debate as to the best way to use glass in greenhouses and conservatories, the building methods had been perfected in both iron and wood, while the industrial revolution had brought into being an expanding middle class. They had the money, the leisure and the lifestyle to enjoy the conservatory. Until now the rare and exotic plants had largely been grown on the estates of the aristocracy, who had also sent out the early plant explorers. But now we were in the early days of the Royal Horticultural Society and the Royal Botanic Gardens at Kew. There was also a growing band of nurserymen who searched the world for plants and could sell them in their thousands to a rapidly increasing urban population.

The comfortable Victorian villas being built for the new middle class were no longer of the severe and symetrical design of the eighteenth century house and could accommodate conservatories, porches, glazed corridors and verandas. The scene was set for the climax of ornamental gardening under glass. The Victorian conservatory was to be fashionable for some fifty years. Incredible glass palaces were built for the very rich, and pre-fabricated conservatories in a multitude of designs were added to so many houses in town and country that ultimately they ceased to be high fashion.

At first there was a tendency to create an indoor garden with paths and even a central lawn. The recent discovery of how to make artificial stone led to a mass of elaborate urns, basins, fountains and statuary. Cast iron was also popular for garden furniture. Tying climbing plants to iron pillars was a major preoccupation and they were also trained over wire balloons and umbrellas. In the larger gardens the practical art of gardening was at its zenith with huge staffs working very long hours and undergoing rigorous apprenticeship. The bowler hat was about to be invented and there are many people still living who remember the rule of the bowler-hatted head gardeners with awe. It was not only the captains of industry who aroused fear in the Victorian age; the master craftsmen were no less demanding.

The great age of glass began to go into decline at the end of the nineteenth century. Changes in sentiment brought a change in taste. Frills and furbelows, Victorian fussiness and extravagance were left behind. The open air became fashionable. With more exercise and simpler clothes women had greater freedom – and did not need a conservatory in which to receive a proposal of marriage!

During the first quarter of the twentieth century the conservatory was in a constant state of decline. Thousands were pulled down as the reduced gardening staffs struggled to maintain the large and elaborate gardens of a bygone age.

Both world wars had catastrophic effects on ornamental plants under glass. Lack of fuel, lack of care and the need to concentrate wholly on the growing of food all took their toll. By the end of the second world war there were extremely few greenhouse plant collections left in Britain. Although the love of gardening soon revived, the ornamental glasshouse did not have a high priority and fuel was still rationed.

Tropical plants, however, did return to favour in the form of 'houseplants'. The craze for these on the continent spread to Britain in the '50s, as our homes gradually became better heated and a wider public was able to afford plants for decoration of the home. Since then there have been great advances in scientific knowledge connected with plant growing under glass, although the effort and technology has been almost wholly concentrated on commercial horticultural interests.

Today we are once more in a difficult financial period. This time it is one that looks like creating far more leisure for more people in the future. Shorter working hours and earlier retirement tend to concentrate attention on improving the home and enjoying interests that can be indulged within it. I do not doubt that many of us will express ourselves in ways that include the growing of plants under glass protection where we can enjoy them at all seasons. No climate is better suited to the conservatory than the temperate climate of Britain.

A point it is easy to lose sight of today is the adventurous excitement of the Victorian period. A very large proportion of the ornamental plants now grown under glass were actually discovered and introduced into this country in Victorian times. Not only were they new but they had been found by our intrepid explorers in the far flung outposts of our glorious Empire and beyond. The plant hunters had faced great hardships and dangers in finding the plants and many of them lost their lives in the search. Even when safely stowed on a ship 90 per cent of the plants were lost. Quite apart from the hazards of storms and pirates, most long sea voyages included two periods in the tropics and severe cold and storms while rounding Cape Horn. It was only in the middle of the century that it was realised that if plants were established in a sealed glass box they had a good chance of surviving the long voyage. The use of the Wardian case, as it was called after its inventor, meant that the more delicate tropical plants and the wonders of China had a chance of surviving the journey. The use of the Wardian case turned the trickle of new introductions into a flood.

3

The Building

It is impossible to build a conservatory in the ideal place. If it is to adjoin the house at a convenient point, there is bound to be a limited choice of position. There are, however, plants suited to every amount of light and degree of temperature. The formidable cost of heating today is likely to affect both the size of the structure and its position. It may also determine its construction if it is to be heated much above freedom from frost in winter. The fiction that double-glazing is uneconomic is beginning to be overcome and it is well worth considering incorporating standard double-glazed units in a structure in which plants are displayed. This is especially true where the conservatory is seen as an additional living space to make entertaining easier. But it is a matter of working out the relative costs of construction and of heating allied, of course, to the total cost. There can also be a rigid plastic lining to a glass exterior and various other forms of insulation to solid parts of the building. Blinds are also sometimes used to reduce heat-loss at night.

Although one feels that by now there must be better and cheaper alternatives to glass, it is in fact very hard to beat. There is no material for a conservatory that transmits light better than glass or is as easy to clean. Glass is a very long-lasting substance so long as it is not shattered by impact or a heavy fall of snow. This latter danger should always be considered when choosing a conservatory. It may be necessary to take some action to prevent snow from slipping off a roof on to the conservatory. Armoured glass is much favoured for roofs.

The recent emergence of reasonably priced conservatories with curved 'glass' roofs is an interesting development. But the curved parts are not in fact glass and so far all the alternatives to glass have been found to deteriorate with age. Nor are the rigid alternatives to glass significantly cheaper. They have advantages for the handyman in being light and easily cut so that the framework can be lighter and have fewer glazing bars. However, the structure will always have to stand up to wind and weather. A major advantage of the new materials is the possibility of twin-walled construction to increase insulation. This is very important as none of the new materials retains heat as well as glass.

At the time of writing twin-walled polycarbonate sheeting is about twice the price of horticultural glass, but the heat-loss is said to be about 40% less than that of single glass. For a heated structure the extra cost of insulation is very quickly recouped in heating costs. The twin-walled materials do, however, cut down on the light, which is serious in winter. They are also not transparent like glass and that greatly reduces their value for conservatory walls.

The more experience one actually has, the harder it becomes to say with any certainty what the best site for a conservatory is. It depends so much on what it is wanted for. Plants can be found to decorate all aspects from north to south and east to west. It is obviously helpful not to be in the teeth of the prevailing wind as it costs so much in heating. Yet a conservatory may have been built to shelter some part of the house from that wind. In that case it is desirable that there is some form of wind-break at a distance from the conservatory on the windward side. The south wall is usually recommended for a lean-to because it is the warmest and has the best winter light. A lean-to on a south wall is, however, very hot in summer and it will be essential to have effective shading. Considerable heat will be saved in winter by the sun shining on the back wall, which stores the warmth to some extent. There is always less light in a lean-to than in a free-standing structure. A position on the north side of a house is liable to receive no sun at all for several months in winter, and this restricts its use and makes it very cold at that time. However, it may be particularly agreeable for use in warm summer weather. Some value a conservatory most for sitting in the sun early in the day. For this an eastern aspect may be good, though it might be exposed to cold winds. On the east side of a house one is in shade after midday, which may be just what is wanted. A conservatory facing west will be sunny at the cocktail hour. This might be considered either delightful or disastrous!

It can be very attractive to look through a conservatory from within the house, if this does not create too much shade in a room in constant use or restrict its ventilation. Another thought is to have a conservatory upstairs in a building or over a garage. Modern materials make this easier than it used to be as one can use both light-weight compost and containers. It is even possible to grow plants entirely by hydroculture, without soil.

Although the actual conservatory one wishes to add to one's home may not concern the authorities, it is unwise today to put up any building without checking on planning permission. The firms which sell the more elaborate conservatories claim to handle this for the customer. Frankly, one cannot be certain what the situation will be in any particular position or locality. In the eyes of the law there are important distinctions between a house extension and a conservatory which affect the way it is rated and allowed to be used.

In Britain building regulations will of course have to be observed, and the local building inspector has to approve any structure being attached to a house. But planning permission is unlikely to be needed if no part of the conservatory projects beyond the building line of the front of the original house or is higher than the house roof. There may, of course, be restrictive covenants in the actual deeds of the house preventing additions being made.

In addition the conservatory must not cover more than half the original garden and, if it is near a boundary, it is limited to a maximum height of 3.90m (13ft). Not surprisingly, one cannot use a conservatory as a separate dwelling without planning permission, and one cannot increase the volume of the original house by more than the permitted limits without planning permission. These limits, if you live in a terraced house, are 149 cubic yards (114 cubic metres) or 10 per cent of the volume of the original house, whichever is the greater. In other cases it can be 15 per cent of the volume of the original house but only up to a total of 149 cubic yards (114 cubic metres). When calculating the size of extensions to the original house, one has to include any that may have been made previously as this is a once-and-for-all allowance.

If you live in a listed building you will need Listed Building Consent, and there may be complications if you are in a conservation area, a National Park or an area of outstanding natural beauty. The regulations are not uniform all over the United Kingdom. Scotland and Central London are notably different. There is a free booklet called *Planning Permission – A Guide for Householders* available from the local planning authority.

If a tenant wishes to put up a glasshouse in such a way that it can be removed at the end of the tenancy, this is a tricky area but not impossible. The building can stand on a row of loose bricks but it must not rest on a foundation of bricks cemented together. There are also circumstances in which it can rest on a back wall so long as it is not secured by nails. Obviously the position needs to be clarified in writing with the landlord and, if necessary, from the local authority.

The cost of a conservatory today can vary enormously from the do-it-yourself affair constructed from second-hand materials to the specially designed building employing an architect. All one can really say with certainty is that it is likely to cost between £500 and £7,000. Unfortunately it would not be difficult to spend £10,000 but if one is building a conservatory instead of an extra room, this can still be worth doing.

The ready-made lean-to greenhouse often used as a conservatory is the simplest option. It comes in a great variety of materials and sizes. There is often a standard width with a choice of length. One must remember that even four chairs and a table with room to walk round them take up a considerable amount of space. If there is to be a door to the house and a door to the garden one can be left with no room for the plants. The safety of the roof is an important point with a lean-to, if there is any danger of tiles falling from above.

In looking for a new conservatory, it is wise to consider all the possible materials and sources of ready-made buildings. The principal manufacturers of conservatories are listed at the end of the book. It may be sensible to choose one that is not too far away though most firms operate anywhere in the country and many have designs which can be put up by local labour. Indeed the foundations usually have to be prepared in advance even if the manufacturer does erect the building.

One cannot make assumptions about the construction of a conservatory from its appearance today. Even if it appears to be of white painted wood in the traditional manner, it is likely that the sash bars will be aluminium. Mercifully the days of putty for glazing are over and the glass will be secured with some form of plastic strip. The upkeep of painted surfaces is now very costly for those who do not do the work themselves. White vinyl-covered aluminium conservatories are one possibility. Aluminium alloy is really the most popular material for ordinary glasshouses today, although when I wrote my first book, I was told with total conviction that it would always be too expensive for such a use. All one can do is to take the best advice available at the time and apply ones own preferences and commonsense to it.

Red cedar is another alternative or even teak if it is custom built. Red cedar is not difficult to maintain and it can also be painted. Whether one wants the conservatory to be brown or white depends very much on its siting. The metal greenhouses and conservatories now come in various forms of anodised colour and can have a bronze appearance.

There are also various types of room extension with glass walls and a wholly or partly solid roof. These are inclined to be ugly as seen from outside but can greatly add to the joys of life as seen from within. There is, however, a magic quality to a well thought-out conservatory that does not ever seem to be achieved with a ready-made house extension.

It is wise to consider both heating and ventilation very seriously before making a final decision on either site or construction. Electricity is certain to be needed, even if only for lighting, and water should be readily available without carrying it through the house. If the heating is to be by oil or coal, there has to be storage for it, and the gas board needs to be consulted about gas.

Although the actual choice of building will probably not be determined by the preferences of the plants, ventilation is a prime consideration. This is the subject most often glossed over or not faced by salesmen and designers generally. It is never safe to assume that what is suggested even by the most famous architect will create an environment in which either people or plants will be comfortable in summer. The purchaser has to exert his or her own imagination to the full. Nothing else will do.

The first choice for the floor of any conservatory is likely to be ceramic or quarry tiles. It is helpful to be able to hose down the floor. This will need a drain. In any case spilled earth, water and mud brought in from outside will have to be coped with.

There are many situations in which a stone floor similar to the terrace outside looks best. An ordinary concrete floor is apt to be dusty and not beautiful, but a well chosen grey paving stone, even if it is of artificial stone, can look very well and also be practical. In some circumstances brightly coloured ceramic tiles may look right but not usually in an old-fashioned kind of conservatory. The Victorians sometimes had terracotta tiles with black designs on them. The floor is very important both visually and practically and needs a great deal of thought. One can have a Portuguese effect of tiles or something cooler in black and white if muddy footsteps are not going to be a feature. If vinyl tiles are contemplated, they need testing first as some of them should carry a health warning for slipperiness when wet. There is also the question of how they are fixed down and whether the method will survive the damp conditions effectively.

4

Temperature and Scope

A conservatory may be part of a home where one hopes to live for half a century, or perhaps merely to pass a single summer. Obviously the time, thought, and skill to be lavished on furnishing it with plants needs to match the circumstances. Some people have a wonderful building with nothing in it while others have a mass of plants and no space to display them. The first thing to be clear about is the climate that you are actually able to provide.

Glass in itself is not an adequate protection against frost in even the warmest parts of the country, and an unheated glasshouse in a cold spell can seem even colder than the outside air. Of course, if the sun shines, the temperature will rise quickly and this alone can spell death to an already frosted plant.

If a conservatory is to be ornamental all the year round, the reality of the winter conditions must be both understood and faced. There are certain risks worth taking. In warm sheltered places and in towns quite tender plants may live through several winters and be well worth growing. However, the risk is there on every frosty night. Many plants survive low temperatures so long as they never actually freeze or if they are kept very dry. The difference between life and death can be as little as a piece of newspaper spread over them on cold nights. Yet most of us if we grow plants at all want them to be healthy rather than struggling to survive. For this it is worth making an informed and careful choice.

It depends on how a conservatory is going to be used, but all of us are likely to want some greenery at all times and many of us also hope for colour for most of the year. If there is no heat at all, the plants that are going to be green in winter will need to be hardy. There can be colour well into the autumn and hardy bulbs start showing their cheerful faces early in the new year. However, unless there is some extra warmth from somewhere, geraniums and the majority of flowering gift plants are likely to die.

In summer the differences between one conservatory and another depend on their position in relation to the sun and how they are managed. From the beginning of May to the end of September the main problem in most conservatories is to keep the temperature down, the plants watered and the atmosphere sufficiently humid for plant life to flourish.

In those months the choice of plants is not difficult and almost everything mentioned in this book will do well, if there is adequate ventilation and a suitable amount of shade. This happy state of affairs comes to an abrupt end in the unheated conservatory with the first frost of autumn. In the north this may come very early, while in the south in exceptional years we might be spared until Christmas. All the same November and December are the darkest, dampest and generally the most difficult months under glass.

The frost-free conservatory has considerably more potential. But to achieve this with any certainty you will need some form of heating. It is a winter haven for half-hardy plants and often in danger of becoming cluttered on that account. The whole world of cacti and succulents is opened up. They are tough plants with undemanding natures. The winter flowers of camellias may be enjoyed without risk of frost damage and we can grow many plants on the borders of hardiness. To be reasonably certain of being free of frost in winter I advise a basic temperature of 4°C (40°F).

Another 3°C (5°F) of heat may double the cost of heating, but this raises the conditions to what is generally described as the 'cool' greenhouse. Although 7°C (45°F) will be the minimum night temperature for much of the time, during the day it will rise several degrees higher by the heat of the sun or just through the radiation from a bright sky trapped by the glass. With a minimum temperature of 7°C (45°F) there is a very wide choice of plants that can be grown successfully and this includes most of those normally thought of as conservatory plants.

If you are able to maintain yet another 3°C (5°F) as your minimum on the coldest night, that is 10°C (50°F), it will be easier to create a genial atmosphere for a wider variety of plants and also to encourage more winter flowers. At this temperature some of the plants more familiarly known as house plants can begin to spread out from the confines of the home and be allowed to grow to a more impressive size. Spring will come even earlier and citrus trees can bear fruit.

A glasshouse where the minimum winter temperature is 13°C (55°F) is generally regarded as 'temperate'. Here one is really in command and can create a more tropical effect if one so wishes. Also many plants will be growing actively all the year round.

If the temperature does not fall below 16°C (60°F) on a winter's night, one is entitled to think of the conservatory as 'warm'. The chances are, that if we choose to maintain such a temperature today, we will be thinking more of people than of plants. The kind of conservatory, or glassed-in space, that is to be used as an extra room all the year round really needs double-glazing or some degree of solid wall or roof to slow down the heat-loss. If the conservatory area is being used seriously as a year-round living space, such as a conservatory-office or glass-walled sitting room, a temperature of 18°C (65°F) is desirable. People sitting around in indoor clothing are not going to feel relaxed and comfortable much below that temperature. However, in these circumstances people are likely to be thinking in terms of wall to wall carpet and this is very far removed from the moist jungle floor! One cannot hose down the carpet on a summer evening and other ways will have to be found to keep a moist atmosphere round the plants that demand it.

At room temperature all the plants we call house plants become possible, so long as one remembers that most of them have been selected for withstanding lack of light indoors. Therefore they will need effective shading from March to October if the sun is going to reach them. There are, however, sun-loving tropical plants that enjoy steady warmth; there are also many flowering shrubs and climbers that could never be grown successfully in an ordinary room.

If a conservatory is going to be devoted to plants rather than people, and the desire is to produce lush tropical growth, a damp atmosphere is the key. Jungle effects are most spectacular using the plants that do need high temperatures, but one can also create the illusion of jungle with the hardier bamboos, gingers, palms, and ferns.

Sometimes a conservatory is wanted as an occasional extra room for parties or other activities and is not going to be heated all the time. It is, of course, the normal day and night temperatures and atmospheric humidity that decide climate and determine what can be grown all the year round. What is added in the summer months depends entirely on how much expense or work or back-up space is available to keep the conservatory going.

A back-up area of some kind is, of course, very helpful. Ideally, if there is a greenhouse, young plants can be raised and those that are 'resting' can do so out of sight. However, a sheltered spot outside, a frame, a shed or even a spare room can all be useful. Another possibility is to put up a small structure like the polythene tunnels used by nurserymen but covered with black plastic windbreak material. This gives shade in summer and some shelter from heavy rain, and in summer it can be useful for standing plants in, such as azaleas and camellias. The less back-up there is, the more the plants need to be either permanently attractive or disposable when past their best. One does not want a long 'off' season in a conservatory, although a completely dry dormant season elsewhere may not be inconvenient.

In a lifetime of looking after pot plants the most successful spot I ever came across for keeping green tropical plants healthy during a summer absence was a north-facing bathroom! Life seemed to remain suspended in a constant moist atmosphere, while in a glasshouse it is always active. Nevertheless, the ability to raise new plants depends on light and warmth as well as constant care. A propagator is an asset wherever you choose to keep it.

5

The Setting

It is worth exploring the whole field of containers and staging before making any decision about the arrangement of plants in a new conservatory. Where people will sit is probably the first consideration, together with where the sun will be at various times of day.

In some buildings white, painted, tiered staging as used in Victorian times is the most effective way of displaying plants. There are modern versions of this which can be made of wood or metal. Where there is less room the traditional white Victorian jardinières made of painted wire can be charming in the right surroundings. It must be remembered that with all forms of open staging, where there is free air movement all round the pots they will dry out very quickly in hot weather. Solid staging on which one can have a damp gravel base or some form of automatic watering may be easier to maintain, though less attractive to look at. Much depends on the scale of the operation. Some arrangement to vary the height of the plants is highly desirable. This can be achieved with hanging baskets, plants on pedestals and climbers on the walls. Tables and jardinières can be of different heights. Tall plants such as standard fuchsias or oleanders can stand on the floor. Even when a conservatory contains very few plants, it does make all the difference to their impact if they are well placed visually and also of the right scale.

Wood can be used to make any size or shape of staging, table or trough that fits the position. Round and square tubs are readily available and also copies of traditional wooden containers in other materials. Wood needs protection if constantly in contact with damp soil, but there is a choice of non-toxic stains for this purpose. One can also have liners inside wooden containers. Where space is limited, the window box shape may be useful.

There are a variety of large self-watering containers of the kind used in hotels and offices, which can enable the bigger plants, or groups of plants to flourish in difficult conditions with little attention. These are usually made of white plastic but once the plants are trailing over the edges this is not noticeable. There are, of course, many large containers designed for other purposes in which plants can be grown.

The ordinary hand-made terracotta flower pot in which everything used to be grown seems to have become almost a status symbol today. I feel quite confused about it myself as nostalgia tangles with ecology, fashion and art. Those active in saving the whale or the golden eagle are less likely to have a plastic flower pot than the rest of us! The truth is that the terracotta flower pot was both cheap and effective in its day and the plastic flower pot is cheap and effective in ours. It is lighter to handle, easier to clean and takes up less space when not in use. The fact that less frequent watering is needed can be helpful. Like many modern inventions the plastic flower pot is convenient, without charm and less long-lasting than we are led to believe. If one likes terracotta enough to use it for everything, there is still plenty to be found. When it comes to large decorative containers there is an enormous choice, at a price. The traditional hand-made Italian terracotta is perhaps the most artistic, but there are also factory-made pots, window boxes, urns and bowls in a multitude of shapes and sizes. I am glad to see that our own British potters have also taken up the challenge in recent years.

Cement is not to be spurned as an alternative, but good designs are hard to find. It is now manufactured in forms light enough to be practical in confined spaces and some would be ornamental in any modern setting. Another possible alternative of special value where weight is important is fibre-glass. This is much more durable than plastic, which becomes brittle in time with exposure to light. There are black fibre-glass reproductions of classical designs that may be suitable where it would be difficult to place a modern object. There are small window boxes, as well as the larger pieces, which are hard to distinguish from the antique lead originals.

In some positions one feels the need for glazed pots. A Devon pottery now makes a variety of wine jars and other large rounded containers in a biscuit-coloured glaze that I find very pleasing. There are also other sources of the Ali-Baba type of jar.

The traditional glazed and decorated Chinese storage jars are once more being imported in various sizes together with other glazed containers, which compare well in price with European products. Genuine Victorian glazed pots and urns are sometimes seen as well as modern reproductions. Portugal and Spain also make their contributions with decorative ceramic wares.

The choice of hanging baskets is more difficult. I am not sure that there is an ideal hanging basket. If one is going to sit under it, the enclosed non-drip type is desirable. The old-fashioned wire basket skilfully planted and lined with moss still has its adherents and there are still a few nurseries prepared to make them up for one in the spring. There is a lot to be said for hanging plants, so long as one recognises that they will need very regular watering in hot weather. There are half-baskets for fixing to walls. One can also suspend individual pots, orchid baskets made of wooden slats, or even pieces of wood with air plants glued or wired on to them. Indeed, artificial trees can be constructed to support epiphytes.

Fountains, pools, rockeries and fern walls are other possible delights, while some consider that the true conservatory should be arranged as an indoor garden with the plants growing in ground beds. This dates from the period when ladies safeguarded their delicate complexions by promenading in the shelter of the 'winter garden'. Ground beds make for a damper atmosphere, which may not always be wanted. However, one or two climbers with their roots in the soil do make it very much easier to give a graceful furnished look to the larger structure.

Personally I sympathise with Shirley Hibberd, the distinguished gardening writer, when he surveyed the conservatory scene a hundred years ago: 'The conservatory is intended for enjoyment and display. Some very humble and in some cases useless glass structures are styled "conservatories," but the term applies properly to an edifice of sufficient size to accommodate camellias and orange trees, and the free movement of full-grown persons attired in a manner which would render it inconvenient for them to come in contact with damp flower pots.'

For those who aspire to a 'Victorian' conservatory there is really nothing more to be said.

6

Heating, Ventilation and Shade

The subject of heating is a difficult and painful one today. Few wish to face the real cost. I have already drawn your attention to the importance of shelter and also to the possibility of double-glazing. With a position adjoining a building there may be considerable protection from the elements and extra warmth coming from a heated building. A conservatory built to protect a house from the prevailing wind in Aberdeenshire, however, will not have the climate one would hope for against a south wall in Cornwall.

The difference between metal and wood construction is fairly slight, although it is sometimes claimed that wood is 10 per cent warmer. When building a conservatory one has to consider the cost of maintenance as well as of heating. I will, however, admit that amateur efforts at lining or double-glazing glasshouses are simpler with a wooden construction.

All conservatories will need some heating if frost is to be excluded with any certainty and it is often implied that an extra radiator on the central heating system will solve all the problems. This can be a costly and ineffective solution unless it is very carefully thought out and executed. Most people turn off their central heating at night, which is just when the heat is most needed. This can be overcome by putting a frost-stat in the conservatory, set to turn the heat on when the temperature falls to a pre-set minimum. This will of course bring on the central heating in the house as well. Conversely, there can be no guarantee of maintaining a particular temperature in a building as poorly insulated as a conservatory over a period of time merely with an extra radiator off a house system controlled by its own internal thermostat. Nor can individual thermostats on each radiator be expected to cope effectively with this problem.

Natural gas is another possible fuel. There are gas heaters designed for greenhouses that are suitable for small structures. As these do not have an outside flue, they are not an ideal form of conservatory heating. Any gas heater has to be approved by the local gas board. They may be willing to lay the necessary service piping more cheaply than a builder. Some of the small heaters can also be used with bottled gas, but this is an expensive and troublesome form of heating. The gas bottles have to be constantly renewed in bad weather when they are most needed. For a fair sized conservatory it may be worth considering a gas-fired balanced flue convector heater. This is wall-mounted and has a small external flue. It does not use the air in the conservatory for combustion and has a non-electric thermostat.

Safety is a factor of great importance when every form of heating has its dangers. The simple oil burner which smokes and blackens every leaf as well as damaging the plants is a fairly common experience. The more sophisticated oil-burning boiler, which blows warm air, is a possibility for large conservatories. But if its chimney becomes blocked for any reason the blackening effect is even more devastating. I have even had such a boiler turn itself off in freezing conditions because the sun on the snow was so bright that this was interpreted by the boiler safety mechanism as a fire in the building and it cut off the boiler's fuel supply! Regular maintenance by a reliable person is important with oil. It must also be remembered that with any form of heating which includes a flame, there must be enough ventilation at all times to keep it burning and prevent fumes.

Even that expensive paragon electricity can play cruel tricks in the testing conditions of a damp glasshouse. It is very important to have electrical work in the conservatory done with the correct cable for use in both damp conditions and sunlight. It also needs checking each year.

I recently had a fire in a greenhouse, caused by a small length of old cable connected to a thermostat. The fuse blew all right but that did not stop the cable continuing to burn. It would have done considerable damage if I had not happened to notice it. All the same, electricity is a clean, easily controlled, and reliable way of heating and the cost depends on the rates obtainable. Most of the electricity will be used at night.

In a small poorly ventilated conservatory there is much to be said for having an electric fan heater which circulates the air all the time and has a built-in thermostat to bring on the heat when the temperature falls. If one is relying on a heater with moving parts running continuously it is wise to have a spare. With every form of electric heating it is essential to have thermostatic control. For a large conservatory it is possible to use warm blown air as used in industry. With all blown air there is a certain degree of noise. One can also have electric tubular heaters designed for greenhouses and rated at 60 watts per foot (30 cm). These have to be fixed to the walls and are more costly to install, but silent.

With modern technology, amazingly complex automatic systems of heat and ventilation control are possible. They may be too costly and it is quite certain that they will not be satisfactory unless the owners themselves have gone into the subject really thoroughly. Only they know how the system is going to be used and it is vital to consider what might happen in extremes of weather or when everyone is away on holiday.

In America, where the climate is generally both hotter and colder than in Britain and money is spent more freely on controlling it, there are elaborate systems of variable-speed fans moving air in and out of buildings according to the temperature. In Britain too it may be worth thinking of the possibility of moving warm air from the house to the conservatory when frost threatens. Adjustable frost-stats and thermostats can be used with extractor fans; Vent-Axia is a firm that has given some thought to this. One may well not want to lose warm air from the house in winter, but where the threat of frost in a conservatory is rare, such a system might be of value when the temperature falls suddenly at night.

Ventilation is as vital a part of temperature control as heating. One has to keep the temperature down when the sun is shining on the glass. Fresh air is also needed for healthy plant growth. There is a tendency to rely too much on doors standing open in summer – though security may make this most unwise. Incredibly, some conservatory manufacturers do not provide roof ventilation on principle. They are fearful of being sued for damage due to leaking roofs. Where there are carpeted floors their alarm may even be justified. I can only say that one would like the openable ventilated area in summer to equal one fifth of the floor area. This is an ideal rarely realised. Nevertheless, roof ventilators should be insisted on for the comfort of both plants and people. Unless they are exceptionally 'large they can be automated quite cheaply. Louvred ventilators let into the side walls, to improve air circulation, can also be automated with adjustable systems depending on the expansion of materials in an enclosed cylinder. Extractor fans can be used for cooling but always make some noise. They can be useful in the absence of the owner.

Shade also has its place in temperature control and is most necessary in the smallest conservatory with the least ventilation. The temperature fluctuates less violently the larger the cubic area, but in most conservatories the majority of plants need some shade from April to October. For coolness the external blind is much the most effective, though rarely used because of its cost. It is also unsuitable on a windy site. Internal blinds are becoming more sophisticated every day. There are many kinds giving different degrees of shade. Any form of thermal blind is likely to pay for itself quite soon in a heated conservatory but is likely to cut out too much light if used regularly in summer or in daytime in winter.

Conservatories used to be shaded by applying a very thin mixture of flour and water to the glass. Today there is a choice of patent mixtures that claim to be easily removed at the end of the season. This is a cheap but often ugly solution. One can also fix up sheets of shading material inside the conservatory and leave it up all through the summer. There is a fine polypropylene netting made for the purpose and other materials of varying thickness sold by the metre. Unfortunately in the British climate there are many overcast days in summer when shading is not wanted. Nevertheless, direct sunshine in the middle of the day is always a danger to plants unless the ventilation is faultless.

Those who entertain in the conservatory after dark may want to have blinds on the side walls for privacy. One way of dealing with this problem is to have louvred blinds made of vertical strips of fibre-glass material which fold away neatly into the corners.

I have deliberately made this a chapter full of gloom and doom to counter the unflagging optimism of salesmen and advertisements. All forms of heating are made to sound so luxuriously simple and trouble-free.

7

Soil and Water

Although it would be possible to devise a special and ideal compost for each individual plant this is quite unnecessary. It is not even attempted nowadays. For most of us the important thing is to be able to use a minimum number of reliable materials that are readily available locally. The choice will depend on how much actual growing will be done and whether seed raising and propagating are part of the plan.

The John Innes potting composts originally devised by the John Innes Institute some fifty years ago are soil-based. They have stood the test of time but vary in quality according to the loam used. Unfortunately good loam is a valuable and diminishing asset and these composts are not always satisfactory although I, personally, continue to prefer them.

The composts come in four forms: seed compost (J.I.S), J.I.P.1, J.I.P.2 and J.I.P.3. Number 1 is for pricking out seedlings and very young plants, number 2 for potting on and re-potting the majority of plants, and number 3 for filling tubs or larger pots of strong-growing or woody plants. They contain more fertilisers the higher the number. They are all sold ready-mixed and should be used when fresh and not stored for long. It is worth checking that each bag has the John Innes Manufacturer's Association mark on it. If it proves unsatisfactory the John Innes Maufacturers Association wish to know.

I find that a large bag of J.I.P.2 is the most useful. To this I add extra sharp sand for everything on any form of automatic watering, and also for all cacti and succulents as well as plants that need very free drainage or a soil that is not too rich.

In case you want to make your own composts, J.I.S. consists of 2 parts by bulk of medium loam mixed with 1 part of granulated peat and 1 part of coarse sharp sand. To each bushel (37 litres) of this mixture is added 1½oz (42g) superphosphate of lime and ¾oz (21g) ground limestone or chalk.

The potting compost is made of 7 parts by bulk of medium loam, 3 parts granulated peat and 2 parts coarse sand. For J.I.P.1 add ¾oz (21g) limestone or chalk and 4oz (113g) John Innes Base fertiliser per bushel (37 litres). The easiest approximation of a bushel is two large buckets full.

The John Innes base (which can be bought ready-mixed) consists of 2 parts by weight superphosphate of lime, 2 parts hoof and horn meal, and 1 part sulphate of potash. For J.I.P.2. double the doses of fertiliser and of ground limestone or chalk. For J.I.P.3 use 12oz (340g) base fertiliser and 2¼oz (63g) ground chalk.

The loam should be sterilised. This means heating it as quickly as possible to 82–93°C (180–200°F) and maintaining this temperature for 10–20 minutes. One can make up composts without sterilising the loam but the results are very much less reliable.

Today most plants are raised commercially in various forms of peat-based compost. These have some advantages over those based on soil. They are lighter to carry, cleaner to use, and can be stored for longer without deteriorating. Their disadvantages are that as plants grow larger they become unstable if there is no weight of soil or a clay pot to keep them upright. The plants will also need more frequent watering and earlier more continuous and more accurate feeding. There is not the same reserve of nutrients as in soil. If I were only going to use bought plants for decoration in a confined space, I would probably use peat-based composts. In a hanging basket soil is better as it dries less quickly.

I think that for most seed sowing peat composts have a slight advantage, but otherwise I usually use soil except for lime-hating plants and those which clearly prefer peat. Peat-based composts are readily available in a multitude of branded forms. These vary according to the type of peat used and whether it is mixed with sand or other substances. The fertilisers used also vary and are apt to include secret ingredients as the firms vie with one another for our custom. It is possible to buy peat-based composts made with slow-release fertilisers which claim to be suitable for everything, including rooting cuttings and seed-sowing.

Many people in fact mix the peat-based composts with the John Innes composts in the hope of getting the best of both worlds. This can be very successful. I often use a half and half mixture. Indeed, there is now a commercial ready-packed compost that is of the John Innes type, but with much less soil so that it is not too heavy to carry home. It is helpful to become familiar with the particular qualities of a locally available compost and one or two useful additives such as sharp sand or perlite.

A lime-free compost is necessary for some ericaceous (i.e. belonging to the *Ericaceae*, or heather, family) and other lime-hating plants such as azaleas and camellias. This compost is usually peat-based and sometimes called 'Ericaceous Compost'.

There are also commercially available ready-made composts for other special categories of plants such as cacti and orchids. The latter have been rescued from their elitist position by the fact that the osmunda fibre, in which they were traditionally grown, became too costly for the trade to use and something simply had to be done. The answer was a combination of various materials which were the unwanted by-products of industry. Surprisingly, many orchids seem to prefer ground bark to osmunda fibre and its use is infinitely simpler. Ground bark comes in many grades and is valued in horticulture as it rots down less quickly than peat and retains an open structure, which suits orchids and epiphytic plants generally. One can buy ready-made orchid potting mixtures in which plastic offcuts, perlite or other artificial materials are added in various proportions. The orchid nurseries usually sell the compost and explain its use. Live sphagnum moss is sometimes used, when available, in composts for both orchids and bromeliads.

You will also find materials which help to create light and porous composts for cuttings and seed-sowing at garden centres. Vermiculite which looks like a pale buff breakfast food and perlite which is a white substance made from volcanic rock are the most commonly seen. These are useful additives particularly where light weight is important. Sand should always be described as sharp and one only needs the one type, though fine grit is a possible alternative.

Another useful material in a conservatory is aggregate. You may think of the gravels used when mixing concrete, and it is true that gravel is a possible material to put on glasshouse benches. There are, however, aggregates used in horticulture which are much lighter in weight and artificially made. These are neutral and sterile and also absorb water. This is helpful in maintaining a moist atmosphere round pot plants standing on benches.

If one is far from a source of supply or does not have a car, it is possible to buy all the necessary materials by mail order in various sizes of bag.

Much sound advice on the use of composts is often printed on each bag but if not the principles are simple enough. Use it in a damp but not soggy condition, avoiding leaving any empty pockets of air round the roots, but never ram it hard. A light firming with the fingers is all that is needed and peat composts need even less firming than soil. Roots need air as well as water which is why they die so quickly in water-logged conditions. Modern plastic pots do not need drainage material at the bottom of the pot.

The compost is only part of the battle as acceptable conditions of moisture and warmth in soil and surroundings play an important part in the life of plants.

Here is a quick run-down on how the composts are used from the cradle to the grave:

Seed Sowing. For this a fine compost is best. It needs to be uniformly damp without being soggy and very lightly pressed down so that the seeds will have contact with the compost. As it is important that a hard pan does not develop on the surface, which might prevent the tiny seedlings breaking through, one tries to arrange things so that there is no over-head watering until the seeds have germinated. This means watering the containers from below and letting them drain before the seeds are sown. Then they are kept covered until the seedlings emerge and need light and air. Never expose seeds or seedlings to direct sunlight.

1. The great early 19th-century conservatory at Bicton.

2. An elegant small modern conservatory built of cedar.

3. A large modern lean-to conservatory.

4. A modern orangery built in the grand style.

5. Inside the conservatory at Bicton.
6. The interior of the orangery shown in Plate 4.

7. A great variety of plants contained in a simple lean-to conservatory.

8. An effective mixture of rare and everyday plants on stepped staging.

Cuttings. Cuttings are a quick and often easy method of propagation and here again it is a disadvantage for the compost to be highly fertilised. A mixture of equal quantities of peat and sharp sand, peat and perlite or even plain vermiculite can all be used. Any of these will enable cuttings to root because they provide well aerated but moist surroundings so long as the cuttings are enclosed in a propagator or a plastic bag. Once they are rooted more nutrients will be needed. The cuttings are then potted up individually in potting compost.

Pricking out. This is the established phrase for lining out young seedlings with space to grow in a larger container. The classic arrangement used to be 5cm (2in) apart in wooden boxes 36 x 20 x 5cm (14 x 8 x 2in). These have been replaced by plastic trays of similar and also much smaller sizes. You can take your pick. In the conservatory, when only a few plants are needed, it may be best to put each seedling in a small pot or in some cases to put several to grow together in a larger pot. J.I.P.1 was devised for this stage in the life of a seedling but it is not really an essential compost to have. Many peat-based composts are now sold designed for all stages in the potting process, and with slow-release fertilisers it is easier to avoid over-feeding young plants.

Potting on. This is the time-honoured phrase for putting a growing plant into a larger pot when the soil in the old pot is exhausted and full of roots. One traditionally pots on until the plant has reached either the largest convenient size or the flowering pot which is big enough for it to give of its best. Modern science has made it possible to keep large plants going in small pots but this needs great attention to feeding and absolutely no failures in watering as small pots dry out so fast. All plants as they grow tend to need a stronger compost and more room for their roots. At the same time there is a definite limit to both the size of the pots and the size of the plants one may be able to accommodate. The fact that a large area of soil with few roots in it soon goes sour if over-watered has made it customary to move plants on, only one or two sizes of pot at a time. This is, however, very much a matter of personal choice. Some plants are unwilling to flower until the pots are very full of roots and others benefit from a free root-run. I have mentioned some particular preferences in my notes about the individual conservatory plants.

Potting back. This has gone out of fashion somewhat as a term but still has its uses. What it means is removing much of the old soil and some of the roots, and re-potting in fresh soil in the same size of pot or even a smaller one than before. This can be done at the end of the summer with regal pelargoniums and fuchsias. They will then take less room in the winter and are potted on again in the spring when they are growing once more. The grouping of plants in a single container often has considerable advantages. They create their own micro-climate of moist air and dry out less rapidly than in smaller pots. One can also replace showy flowering plants while retaining more permanent evergreen foliage. Some people keep the individual plants in pots buried in peat, while others plant them out. If the container has a self-watering system, maintenance of such a group is very simple.

This brings me to the subject of watering which seems to cause so much trouble and heart-searching. There is a considerable gulf of understanding between those who water plants to save them from an early death and those who are consciously endeavouring to imitate the rainfall pattern of some distant native habitat. I hope that conservatory owners will take a middle course of regularity and watchfulness. It is impossible to give rule of thumb instructions of the 'once a day' or 'once a week' kind. Temperature, atmospheric moisture, time of year, size of plant, and size of pot are just a few of the things which affect the consumption of water. Our plants are with us to look attractive in their chosen setting, in a particular building and for a relatively short time. They are 'on show' and the show must go on even if the plants have to be replaced. If they are native to dry or freely draining conditions (such as a mountain, a cliff or semi-desert), they will be totally unable to stand prolonged saturation. Indeed, very few plants can endure stagnant moisture. This is mainly because it excludes the necessary oxygen from the soil. Obviously the tips of the roots should never be bone dry though the surface of the soil is a different matter. Those who watch their plants closely will learn to recognise when the leaves are just begining to be held in an attitude which denotes lack of moisture. Wilting is never a good thing. But if it has happened neither prolonged sogginess nor constant guilty driblets of water are the answer. The roots will be recovering from damage and liable to rot.

Plants usually respond best to a thorough watering which wets the whole of the soil in the pot, followed by a similar watering before they show any sign of flagging but when the surface of the soil has had time to dry out. Naturally when plants are resting in winter their needs for water will be very much less. If the temperature is low, it is always safer to give a minimum of water and to do the watering early in the day. Generally speaking everything that encourages a damp atmosphere in winter is undesirable unless you are maintaining a temperature of 13°C (55°F) or more, while in summer it is hard to keep enough moisture in the atmosphere as the temperature rises. If you have conditions in which it is possible to damp down the floor night and morning in warm weather it is helpful.

If it is important to give the right amount of water, you may ask yourself, why do plants often do so well when there is constant moisture from automatic watering systems? I think the answer to this is that plants are very adaptable within limits, but they cannot adjust either to days of total neglect or to standing for long in a saucer of water. They suffer from both forgetfulness and guilt but can adapt to a great variety of consistently poor conditions. Most of the plants we grow are in fact hybrids which have been bred to survive what people demand of them. Species on the other hand may only be ideally suited to some very special situation in a few square miles in the southern hemisphere.

8

Pest Control

By far the most important thing about pests is to avoid having them in the first place. In a conservatory one is usually starting with a clean area in which there are no plant pests. These are likely to arrive with the plants themselves and the higher the temperature the more quickly they will multiply. If an old conservatory is being refurbished, it is another story and every effort must be made to cleanse it really thoroughly before the plants are introduced. Scrubbing down the empty building and fumigating it with sulphur candles would be best. This may be quite impractical in a conservatory connected to the house. If plants are already growing in the ground and cannot be removed, a scrubbing down of the building with soft soap and a spraying of the plants with a general insecticide will have to suffice. Soil in ground beds is better replaced if possible. Everything in the conservatory is a potential home for some form of wild life and we do not want those that disfigure plants.

It is wise to remove the plants and to clean out the building once a year. The early autumn may be the best time to do this, as the plants can stand outside while it is done and pests are prevented from over-wintering. Obviously one does not want either to fumigate or to spray noxious chemicals in a building adjoining the home unnecessarily and their lingering smell is often unpleasant. Unfortunately many pests become resistant in time to whatever substance is used. For this reason it is a good idea to vary the cure.

There are now biological predators that one can introduce to eat up some of the most undesirable creepy-crawlies. For these to work well a temperature around 20°C (69°F) is necessary to keep them active. They also need to be introduced at an early stage of the infestation or they may never gain control. At the same time there have to be enough pests to keep the predators feeding happily! Obviously the top priority is to examine every new plant minutely and to keep it isolated at first, if practicable. Two weeks is enough to produce another generation of almost anything and the places to look for trouble are the backs of the leaves, the growing points, and any little corners where branches or leaves join the main stem.

If the more innocuous remedies do not work I destroy the infested plant. People vary very much in their attitudes to these things and some are even willing to have an electric vaporiser disseminating pesticides and fungicides continuously. However, every garden centre is full of less drastic remedies. Fortunately healthy plants are not so vulnerable to all the ills as unhealthy ones, and it is often better to burn a sickly plant rather than to spend time identifying the trouble. It is nevertheless well worth learning to recognise the common pests in order to get rid of them before they become established:

Ants. We all know ants. They need to be discouraged because they 'milk' greenfly and transport them from plant to plant. This is bad in itself and also tends to spread virus diseases. Ants sometimes make nests in pots standing on the floor. There are proprietary ant killers if necessary.

Aphids. These are greenfly and actually come in a variety of colours. They concentrate on the softest and most succulent parts of the plant and can be washed off when first seen but quickly build up to menacing numbers. Derris and pyrethrum and the newer resmethrin would be my first choice. There are systemic insecticides, which are absorbed into the sap of the plant and are effective against all sucking insects, but they are not materials that I am keen to have in my own home.

Mealybugs. These resemble minute pale woodlice and protect their eggs with white wool, which is usually the first thing to be noticed. They are most partial to cacti and succulents, which are otherwise pest-free, but spread to other plants where they choose the backs of the leaves and hidden corners on woody stems. I keep some methylated spirits and a paint brush ready to destroy them without spoiling the appearance of cacti or succulents. In the very early stages mealybugs can be controlled by picking off or crushing them individually.

Red spider mites. These are a serious pest and so small that they are barely visible. They settle on the undersides of the leaves which become bleached by their depredations. A bad infestation leads to a mass of tiny webs under the leaves and very unhappy plants. They do not like to be wetted and are a sign of too dry an atmosphere. Shrubs and carnations are most at risk. Malathion is probably the most commonly used remedy, but they quickly build up resistance. The name of the biological predator used against red spider is *Phytoseiulus persimilis.* It comes on pieces of leaf which can be pinned to the leaves of badly affected plants.

Scale insects. These remain unnoticed until they reach the stage when they build a covering over themselves which makes them resistant to attack. Brown scale is often found on the stems and the backs of the leaves of evergreen greenhouse shrubs. If there are only a few they can be scraped off. They are sucking insects and vulnerable to malathion and systemic insecticides. A sooty mould on the surface of the leaves often betrays their presence.

White fly. This is another serious pest. The minute snow-white flies rise from the plant when it is touched. These are only the final stage of the pests, which as small circular green scales have already been sucking the life-blood from the backs of the leaves. Fuchsias and regal pelargoniums are particularly suscep-tible. It takes repeated sprayings to rid a plant of this pest, because the eggs are not vulnerable and are laid in large numbers. Spraying with permethrin, resmethrin or malathion are some of the options. Biological control is done with a minute wasp called *Encarsia formosa*. Leaves with scales of white fly already invaded by the larvae of the wasp are introduced into the conservatory. This form of control will not survive the winter. Predators are advertised in the gardening press in early summer. It is quite an expensive exercise, but interesting.

When we talk of plant diseases we actually mean the troubles that are not caused by pests or nutritional imbalance. Virus diseases affect a number of plants and cause a streaky or mottled appearance of the leaves. If the latter are held up to the light, they may show distinctive round spots. There may also be distortion of the growth and flowers are affected. The plant is always permanently weakened and there is no simple cure. If one seriously suspects virus, it is much better to destroy the plant before it spreads. Good cultivation sometimes masks the effect of virus, but it is usually obvious in early spring. Avoid taking cuttings in doubtful cases. Zonal pelargoniums and other plants that have been raised from cuttings through many generations are the most frequent victims.

The moulds and the mildews usually leave one alone unless growing conditions are poor. If it is damp and stuffy when the temperature is low, botrytis (often called grey mould) is likely to be seen. Zonal pelargonium leaves and all flower petals or dying vegetation are particularly vulnerable. Modern fungicides such as Benomyl are quite effective, but adequate ventilation and good cultivation are better. Some people have a great deal of trouble with seedlings collapsing because of a fungus known as 'damping off'. Watering the compost with Cheshunt Compound before sowing the seeds or pricking out is a routine precaution one can take.

Mildews are more unpredictable. There are powdery mildews, which create a white powdering on the surface of the leaf, and downy mildews which are more destructive. Both consist of a fungus growth, encouraged by variable temperatures in damp conditions. Begonias, chrysanthemums, cinerarias and roses are likely subjects, and it is worth spraying with Benomyl as soon as the mildew is seen.

Finally, it is good to remember that all that moves should not be attacked in the conservatory. Spiders, hoverflies, ladybirds and toads are hard-working allies which are not always made as truly welcome as they deserve to be.

9

Sources of Plants

Choosing the plants to include in this book has been very difficult. It is frustrating to suggest plants that may exist but are not available commercially. At the same time there are a few plants which are quite common and freely exchanged between friends, but not generally on sale, while others that were everywhere a few years ago do not seem to be anywhere now.

There are plants to be bought as seeds, seedlings, rooted cuttings, young plants, mature plants, dry bulbs, and growing bulbs – not to mention the seeds, cuttings, scales, bulbils and other oddments passed from hand to hand.

Virtually every part of Britain has nurseries, garden centres, chain stores and florists shops which sell plants. There are also many gardens that sell plants on their open days. Charities have plant sales, and countless horticultural societies have occasions when many good plants and cuttings are exchanged.

The specialist nurseries are an important source of the best kinds and greatest diversity of many favourite plants. Bromeliads, bulbs, cacti and succulents, carnations, chrysanthemums, ferns, fuchsias, nerines, orchids, palms, pelargoniums (geraniums) and saintpaulias all have nurseries devoted to the one family or type of plant. They are mostly well worth a visit and many of them sell by mail order.

There are several paper-back garden directories which list nurseries by county and plants by name. As these volumes are not updated each year, it is worth trying to get hold of the most recently published. The specialist societies are another source of both knowledge and plants for those who have a particular interest. They cover the same subjects as the specialist nurseries. With time, however, their addresses change, as their honorary officers are replaced; in Britain the Royal Horticultural Society (80 Vincent Square, London SW1P 2PE) will always help to locate them.

The horticultural magazines contain much sound advice and many advertisements to do with cultivation under glass. Regrettably at the time of writing there is no publication devoted solely to greenhouses and conservatories. For the conservatory owner the most inspiring pictures and decorative suggestions are more often found in the glossy monthlies devoted to the home.

Garden centres are perhaps the most widely spread source of conservatory plants today. The tender plants now sold in quantity are mostly destined for use in the home, and it has become harder to find those able to stand the rigours of unheated or cool conservatories. There are an increasing number of very small nurseries, often started as a hobby, which tend to go in for the more unusual (and often slightly tender) plants. Some of the best local sources depend very much on personal recommendation, which can take time to reach the newcomer to a district.

As I write, the recognition of how many original species and valued older hybrids are in danger of being lost has led to various forms of conservation. Efforts are being made by a number of organisations in Britain to preserve the more unusual plants and to distribute them more widely. The National Council for the Conservation of Plants and Gardens (NCCPG) has its headquarters at the Royal Horticultural Society Gardens at Wisley in Surrey. It has active groups in most counties which have full knowledge of all the nurseries in their area.

Incredibly today it is often easier to buy a tender plant that is a native of Africa, hybridized in Germany, grown in the West Indies and flown to Britain, than one that has spent the whole of its short life in a British glasshouse. The cost of labour, the cost of fuel, and the amount of government subsidy are crucial to profitability in the nursery industry. Therefore raising tropical pot plants in a naturally warm climate with cheaper labour can more than cover the extra transport costs. All these factors tend to change from year to year but it is hardly surprising that the mini plant and the chemical control of plant growth are popular, as plants increasingly travel in containers and finally come home with the groceries. Today it is the buyers for the big chain stores and garden centres who are in the positions of power to insist on high standards of cultivation and to choose what will be grown in quantity.

Although this book includes more than 300 genera (or groups) of plants and many more species and hybrids, this is but a fraction of the possible plants from all over the world that individuals might find worth growing. All the same my selection does include those plants which are obtainable in Britain and generally believed to be the most rewarding and decorative in the conservatory or garden room.

A conservatory is mainly for the enjoyment of the owners who can make a success of growing almost anything they care about. There was a time when many of our hardy plants were grown in conservatories, because they were excitingly new and their hardiness had not yet been tested. Delphiniums, for instance. It would in fact be hard to imagine anything more splendid than delphiniums in flower in May under glass. Hardy shrubs were also forced in heat and then brought into the cooler conservatory to be displayed in flower. Tree paeonies were long believed to be tender and with their beautiful leaves early in the season they might be rewarding still. One of the most vivid memories of the survivors of the ill-fated Tsarist court was of the scent of lilac bushes in the palace rooms before the Russian winter had relaxed its grip.

Plants do not have to be rare or expensive to make a memorable display. Owners with more time than money do not have to look further than a really good seed catalogue to find a wide choice of plants with which to fill the largest conservatory.

The cost of plants depends on rarity, ease of propagation, the need for high temperatures and the rate of growth. Every day costs money. In addition there is the glamour of the 'new,' which often allows a higher price. Whether it is new to science, new to commerce or new to you hardly matters!

In the dictionary of plants that follows I have endeavoured to give the minimum winter temperatures (MWT) needed for the health of each plant that cannot be expected to survive in unheated glass. In doing this one has to take some risks and make some compromises. If a plant is unusually difficult and expensive, there is no point in urging people to grow it at too low a temperature, whereas easier plants are more worth risking. Obviously the position of the conservatory greatly affects the day-time temperatures in winter which should be, and normally are, well above the minimum at which the heating is set. Each year is different, and prolonged spells of high wind and extreme cold upset the best laid plans. It is impossible to define precisely what degree of shelter and artificial heat will achieve freedom from frost in all winters. I have chosen the set temperature of 4°C (40°F) as a suitable aim for the frost-free conservatory since it allows a degree of error and is a popular choice for a variety of reasons.

10

Dictionary of Plants

ABUTILON (*Malvaceae*)
MWT 4°C (40°F). Shrubs from South America that flower for many months. These are quick-growing plants useful in the border or hanging baskets when young. Increase by seed which flowers the first year, or cuttings of half-ripe shoots in June or July. Some are becoming rare and may only be found in private collections. There are hybrids with red, orange, yellow and white flowers, 1.2–1.5m (4–5ft) (*Plate 16*). A. *insigne*, white flowers with red veins in winter. A. *megapotamicum* (syn. A. *vexillarium*) red and yellow, summer. A. *milleri*, yellow flowers suffused with carmine, continuous flowering. A. *striatum* 'Thompsonii', mottled green and yellow foliage, orange flowers. A. *'Savitzii'*, with white markings on the leaves.

ACACIA (*Leguminosae*)
MWT 4°C (40°F). Evergreen flowering shrubs or trees from Australia, valued for their yellow flowers in winter or spring. Prune when necessary immediately after flowering and re-pot every other year in summer. They can be plunged outside in summer but should never be allowed to get dry. All can be raised from seed which should be chipped before sowing. A. *armata* and A. *drummondii* are smaller and slower than most and good for pots. The larger kinds are very fast-growing and soon outgrow a tub. There are now many to choose from at a specialist nursery. All have fluffy yellow flowers but the leaves vary greatly. Keep in full sun and water freely except in cold winter weather. A. *armata*, slow-growing to 3m (10ft), A. *drummondii*, lemon yellow; A. *baileyana* and A. *dealbata* (florist's mimosa), silver leaves and golden flowers, tall; A. *verticillata* (prickly Moses), tiny dark green leaves, pale yellow flowers.

ACALYPHA (*Euphorbiaceae*)
MWT 16°C (60°F). Shrubs from tropical Asia only suitable for really warm moist conditions in good light. A. *hispida* (the Chenille plant, *Plate 17*) with flowers like red worms made of candlewick, is very handsome. A. *wilkesiana* cultivars have brilliantly coloured coppery leaves of little artistic merit. Grow in soil-based compost and re-pot yearly in spring. Increase by tip cuttings in a propagator in spring. Ultimately to 1.8m (6ft).

ACHIMENES (*Gesneriaceae*)
MWT 10°C (50°F) when in greenhouse. Attractive summer flowering plants from South America. The dry rhizomes are planted in spring 2.5cm (1in) deep and about five to a 13cm (5in) pot. They can be started into growth in damp peat and transplanted when 5cm (2in) high. They appreciate warmth and moisture while growing and may need support. The tiny scaly tubers increase naturally and are best kept through the winter quite dry in their pots indoors. There is a wide choice of hybrids in many shades of purple, red, pink, violet and white from 15–38cm (6–15in).

ACORUS (*Araceae*)
MWT 4°C (40°F). A small tufted foliage plant that is virtually hardy. This is one of the few plants that can stand in a saucer of water and must never be dry. Increase by dividing the clump in spring. A bright but not sunny situation and soil-based compost with feeding in summer suits it. *A. gramineus* 'Variegatus, up to 46cm (18in); and a dwarf form *A. g.* 'Albovariegatus', 15cm (6in).

ADIANTUM (*Adiantaceae*)
The maidenhair ferns have a world-wide distribution. Their delicate fresh green fronds are popular everywhere. *A. pedatum*, the North American maidenhair, is the only really hardy one. *A. venustum* from the Himalayas is fairly hardy and our native *A. capillus-veneris* and its many varieties less so. There are hundreds of species and it is difficult to know what one is buying but those most readily available flourish in shade and warmth with a minimum of 13°C (50°F). For cultivation, see FERNS.

AECHMEA (*Bromeliaceae*)
MWT 10°C (50°F). This attractive grey-leaved urn plant is only one of a large family but is often received as a present. The pink bracts last for months.It is an epiphyte living in trees in nature and needs good drainage with moisture and shade in summer and rather dry in winter unless in a warm room. Keep the urn full of water (preferably rain water). *A. fasciata* (syn.*A. rhodocyanea*) (*Plate 18*), pink bracts, small blue flowers. 46cm (18in). For cultivation, see BROMELIADS.

AEONIUM (*Crassulaceae*)
MWT 4°C (40°F). Shrubby succulents from the Canary Islands with rosettes of fleshy leaves on woody stems. A useful foliage plant in cool conditions. Pot in spring in J.I.P.2 with extra sharp sand or grit. Water freely in spring, less toward the end of summer and through winter. Cuttings root easily. Mature shoots ultimately flower and die. *A. arboreum*, best known in its purple leaved variety; *A. haworthii*, blue-green leaves with red edges; *A. undulatum*, slow-growing on a single stem, all about 60cm (2ft). *A. tabulaeforme* forms a flat pale green rosette.

AESCHYNANTHUS (*Gesneriaceae*)
MWT 16°C (60°F). Trailing plants with glossy fleshy leaves and handsome tubular flowers. They are suitable for hanging baskets in warm spacious conditions. They need semi-shade and a moist atmosphere. The flowers are born on the tips of the branches so young plants need pinching back to make them bushy. Some pruning back can be done immediately after flowering. Increase by tip cuttings in a propagator in spring. A. *lobbianus*, very dark green leaves and red flowers: A. *pulcher* rather similar: A. *speciosus* with orange flowers is the most showy and readily available. Their branches may be 60cm (2ft) long.

AGAPANTHUS (*Liliaceae*).
Cold or frost-free. These fleshy-rooted perennials from South Africa are hardy in much of the country. The evergreen kinds certainly need protection in winter. They are good tub plants and have handsome heads of blue or white flowers in summer. Pot the roots in spring singly in a 23cm (9in) pot or grouped in a tub in any loam-based compost. Water freely when growing but very sparingly in winter. Feed before flowering and only re-pot when very pot-bound. Seed sown in spring should flower in the third summer. A. *africanus*, evergreen, blue: A. *campanulatus*, deciduous, blue: A. *praecox* (syn. *umbellatus*) evergreen, pale blue or white. Those known as the 'Palmer hybrids' are the hardiest, 60cm–1.2m (2–4ft).

AGAPETES (*Ericaceae*)
MWT 7°C (45°F). Unusual and rather difficult evergreen ericaceous shrubs with charming waxy bell flowers early in the year. They need a peaty lime-free compost and a moist atmosphere. They come from the Himalayas and China. They are best grown in a tub and trained upwards as the flowers hang beneath the branches. Increase by cuttings in summer. A. *macrantha*, white with delicate red markings. A. *serpens* (formerly *Pentapterygium serpens*), red flowers with darker markings.

AGAVE (*Agavaceae*)
Cold or frost-free. Tough Mexican succulents. Most grow too quickly to keep indoors for long and they have dangerous points at the tips of their sword-shaped leaves. Pot in J.I.P.2 with added grit. Keep all-but dry in winter unless grown in warmth. Water freely April to September. A. *americana* 'Variegata' and A. *v.* 'Medio-picta' are impressive but soon grow too big; A. *angustifolia*, grey-green and smaller; A. *filifera*, dark green; A. *victoria-reginae*, a slow-growing and fascinating plant with very dark green leaves with white markings but needs a MWT of 10°C (50°F).

AGLAONEMA (*Araceae*)
MWT 13°C (55°F). Foliage plants from tropical Asia with attractively marked leaves for warm conditions with no direct sunlight. They have Arum-type

flowers followed by red berries and ultimately form a stem. Grow in soil-based compost and re-pot in spring when really pot-bound. Increase by removing basal shoots with some roots in spring. They like a humid atmosphere. *A. commutatum* and its varieties with deep green leaves with silvery markings: *A. costatum*, a smaller plant: *A. pictum*, deep green leaves marbled grey and white.

ALBIZZIA (*Leguminosae*)
MWT 7°C (45°F). Deciduous flowering tree from central Asia which can be trained against a sunny wall. Like a pink acacia it needs similar treatment. Grow in a border or a tub. Sow seed in warmth in early spring. *A. julibrissin* and *A. j.* var. *rosea* (brighter pink), summer.

ALLAMANDA (*Apocynaceae*)
MWT 18°C (65°F). Handsome evergreen tropical climbers from South America with yellow bell flowers for much of the year in warmer climates. They need full light and space. Grow in a border of rich well-drained soil. Water freely in summer but little in winter. Feed generously if grown in a tub. Cut back in early spring. Cuttings of young shoots root in a propagator. *A. cathartica* 'Grandiflora' and *A. c.* 'Hendersonii' with brownish buds before the yellow flowers open are the most often seen. *A. neriifolia* is smaller in all its parts and more of a scandent shrub.

ALOE (*Liliaceae*)
MWT 7°C (45°F). Succulent plants from Africa, many with flame-coloured flowers when mature. Shade from full sun in summer. *A. aristata*, miniature rosette plant and almost hardy. *A. ferox* (*Plate 19*), light green spine-edged leaves; *A. variegata* (partridge-breasted aloe), prettily marked leaves. For cultivation, see SUCCULENTS.

ALOYSIA see LIPPIA

AMARYLLIS see HIPPEASTRUM

AMPELOPSIS (*Vitaceae*)
MWT 7°C (40°F). Deciduous climber or trailer with elegant variegated leaves. Pot in J.I.P.2 in spring and re-pot yearly unless in a large container. Cut hard back when leaves fall. *A. heterophylla* 'Elegans', leaves with pink and white markings.

ANANAS (*Bromeliaceae*)
MWT 18°C (65°F). The pineapple has a variegated form and also close relatives used as house plants while young. These handsome spiny plants need warmth, moisture and strong light. They can stay in small pots for several years but all but *A. nanus* will become too big for comfort in four or five years. *A. bracteatus* 'Striatus' (*Plate 20*), leaves striped with cream and suffused with

pink: *A. comosus* (syn. *sativus*) 'Variegatus', green with white margins: *A. nanus*, can bear small inedible green fruit in a 10cm (4in) pot.

ANTHURIUM (*Araceae*)
MWT 18°C (65°F). Flowering plants from tropical America with long-lasting flowers like red plastic. Shade and humidity are essential. Use a peat compost and feed regularly. Re-pot each spring. This is a good subject for soil-less cultivation. *A. scherzerianum* hybrids are the hardiest and most compact.

APHELANDRA (*Acanthaceae*)
MWT 16°C (60°F). Small evergreen tropical shrub known as the zebra plant. Miserable if dry or chilled. A plant for the careful in a warm, bright but not sunny spot. Water freely when in flower and keep just moist for winter rest. Cut back in March and re-pot in April. This is a plant for which I would use half soil-based and half peat compost. *A. squarrosa* with showy yellow flowers and bracts. There are various forms bred for compactness such as *A. s.* 'Louisae,' and *A. s. 'Brockfield'*.

APOROCACTUS (*Cactaceae*)
MWT 10°C (50°F). Epiphytic cactus from Mexico known as the rat's tail cactus because of its trailing stems. It prefers lime-free soil. Water freely in summer but keep barely moist in winter. Good in a hanging basket or wall pot. *A. flagelliformis (Plate 21)*, trailing stems, clusters of red or pink flowers in spring. There are hybrids which are usually more tender.

ARALIA see DIZYGOTHECA and FATSIA

ARAUCARIA (*Araucariaceae*)
MWT 7°C (45°F). Elegant tropical conifer known as the Norfolk Island pine. It makes an attractive and tolerant pot plant with tiered branches and can be used as a miniature Christmas tree. Grow in J.I.P.2 and feed when in active growth. Water freely in summer, rather less in winter. Give some shade in summer. *A. heterophylla* (formerly *A. excelsa*), slow-growing tree.

ARDISIA (*Myrsinaceae*)
MWT 10°C (50°F). Small evergreen shrubs from the tropics with long-lasting red berries in winter. Grow in J.I.P.2 and re-pot yearly in spring. Feed when in active growth and water freely, less in winter. Side-shoots with a heel can be used as cuttings. *A. crenata* (often wrongly called *A. crispa*) grows slowly to 90cm (3ft).

ARISTOLOCHIA (*Aristolochiaceae*)
MWT 13°C (55°F). Perennial climbers with curious spotted flowers for those who like the weird and wonderful. There is one hardy one, *A. macrophylla* (syn. *A. sipho*, Dutchman's pipe) with brown and yellow flowers but *A. elegans* (calico flower) from Brazil and *A. grandiflora* (pelican flower) from

Guatemala are more worthy of room under glass. They need warmth, humidity, shade and rich soil. They can be raised from seeds sown in spring or by cuttings of young shoots in summer. Grow in J.I.P.3 or similar compost, potting on to a 28cm (10in) pot which will prevent them from spreading too much in a border. Water freely in summer and give tomato fertiliser to encourage flowering. Water sparingly in winter. Re-pot in spring.

ARUM LILY see ZANTEDESCHIA

ARUNDINARIA see BAMBOOS

ASCLEPIAS (*Asclepediaceae*)
MWT 10°C (50°F). Tender perennial from tropical America that can be flowered from seed in the first season if sown in warmth in February. Pot singly in J.I.P.1. They prefer a lime-free compost but this is not essential. Nipping out the tips of the shoots makes a bushier plant. Give plenty of water in summer but keep rather dry in winter. Cut back and re-pot each spring. *A. curassavica*, orange flowers, autumn, up to 90cm (3ft).

ASPARAGUS (*Liliaceae*)
MWT 7°C (45°F). Useful foliage plants known as asparagus ferns although they are tuberous and mostly have needle-like foliage. Grow in J.I.P.2 or other soil-based compost and re-pot yearly in spring. The flowers are insignificant but some may have red berries. *A. asparagoides* (syn. *A. medeoloides*) is smilax a twining trailer or climber with *A. a. 'Myrtifolius'* similar but much smaller; *A. densiflorus* 'Myers' is a plume-like form of the familiar *A. d.* 'Sprengeri' much used in hanging baskets; *A. falcatus* has wider leaves and a more shrubby appearance; *A. setaceous* (syn. *A. plumosus*) is the florist's asparagus fern for posies. This is an evergreen climber and can be trained up a wall. There is a miniature form for small pots.

ASPIDISTRA (*Liliaceae*)
MWT 4°C (40°F). The Victorian foliage plant which endures shade and neglect. Grow in any compost. Re-pot only occasionally and feed sometimes. Increased by division in spring. *A. lurida* and its variegated form, glossy leaves and insignificant flowers.

ASPLENIUM (*Asplediaceae*)
Evergreen ferns with shiny pale green fronds used as house plants in warm and bright conditions without sunlight. For soil and cultivation, see FERNS. *A. bulbiferum* (hen and chicken fern) comes from Australia and New Zealand and is happy with MWT 10°C (50°F). *A. nidus* (bird's nest fern) has entire fronds and grows on tropical trees in nature and needs 16°C (60°F). See also FERNS.

ASTROPHYTUM (*Cactaceae*)
MWT 7°C (45°F). A small group of Mexican cacti with few spines and a decorative shape. Buy in spring and re-pot when necessary in a cactus compost

or J.I.P.2 with added coarse sand. Grow in full sun. Water regularly in summer but keep almost dry in winter. These cacti though globular have distinctive ribs and all have yellow flowers when mature. They can be grown from seed but take five years to become impressive. *A. asterias*, no spines,; *A. capricorne*, curly spines; *A. myriostigma*, silvery, no spines; *A. ornatum*, silvery with dark brown spines on ribs.

AZALEA see RHODODENDRON

BAMBOOS
The plants known collectively as bamboos come under the names *Arundinaria*, *Bambusa*, *Phyllostachys* and *Sasa*. They come from places as far apart as the Mediterranean and New Zealand as well as Japan and the whole of tropical Asia. Where there is room for something tall and graceful, large pots or tubs of bamboo can create a tropical atmosphere in virtually any temperature. They all need plenty of water at the roots and generally prefer humidity and shade. Pot or divide in spring and grow in soil-based compost with added leaf-mould (if available) and sand. Feed when growing and give less water in winter. What to grow is a matter of size, hardiness and availability. *Arundinaria fortunei* 'Variegata', striped with silver,tender, 60cm (2ft); *A. nitida* is hardy and elegant, ultimately 1.8m (6ft); *A. pygmaea*, a miniature; *Phyllostachys nigra* has black stems, 2.7m (9ft); *Sasa fortunei* 'Variegata' is quite small and tender. All the bambusas need MWT 10°C (50°F) and the rest like MWT 7°C (45°F) although many will survive without heat.

BAUERA (*Saxifragaceae*)
MWT 4°C (40°F). Small neat Australian evergreen shrub flowering in late winter and spring. Grow in lime-free compost and do not let them get pot-bound until they are fully grown. They can be plunged outside in summer. Increase by half-ripe cuttings in warmth in spring. *B. rubioides*, red, pink or white. 30–60cm (1–2ft).

BEAUCARNEA (*Liliaceae*)
MWT 10°C (50°F). A Mexican desert plant with a swollen base to the stem and a tuft of narrow curving leaves on top. Mature specimens are highly decorative and little trouble. Characteristically we call it pony tail plant and the Americans call it bottle palm. Grow in J.I.P.2 with additional sharp sand. Water moderately in summer and keep all but dry in winter. Feed occasionally in summer. It is easily killed by winter watering. *B. recurvata* (syn. *Nolina recurvata*) ultimately several feet tall in the wild.

BEGONIA (*Begoniaceae*)
MWT 10°C (50°F) for most begonias. All begonias really need an average of 13°C (55°F) to flourish. This is a vast family of tender tuberous, herbaceous and even shrubby plants grown for flowers and foliage. They are very important in

the warm and shaded conservatory or garden room. Without heat the tuberous large-flowered hybrids, also 'Multiflora' and 'Pendula' hybrids, can be started into growth in warmth indoors in spring and used to decorate the conservatory when a night temperature of 10°C (50°F) can be assured. There are also species with tuberous roots that can be kept dry in winter. B. *sutherlandii* with trailing stems and small orange flowers is an easily grown example.

The fibrous rooted B. *semperflorens* in its many strains as used for bedding and pots can be in flower from May to November if bought as young plants. They can be raised from seed at 16°C (60°F) but need care and an early start. Those used for bedding can be potted to go on flowering through the autumn but will not survive the winter under 10°C (50°F). B. *metallica (Plate 23)* has attractive heart-shaped leaves and pink-flushed white flowers.

The pink winter-flowering begonias which look rather similar are called 'Gloire de Lorraine' begonias. These are raised from cuttings in heat in February and are quite tricky to grow as they need abundant atmospheric moisture as well as warmth all the year.

The most familiar winter-flowering begonias today are the recently introduced 'Rieger' begonias. These are semi-tuberous and grown commercially with artificially adjusted day length. They come in all the warm colours and are on sale in flower most of the year. They can be increased by rooting a leaf with half its stalk buried in an equal mixture of sand and peat in a propagator. These too need shade from summer sun.

The ornamental-leaved Rex begonias need shade always and like a moist atmosphere, as do the smaller B. *boweri* cultivars with fringed and brown speckled leaves.

The large cane-stemmed begonias become shrub-like in time and can be planted out in a warm conservatory. B. *coccinea* and 'President Carnot' are two to look out for. A species from Mexico, B. *fuchsioides (Plate 22)*, with small red flowers and a long flowering season in early summer is one of the best in a conservatory and can be trained against a wall.

Peat-based potting mixtures can be used for begonias which like a spongy soil. I find it better to mix soil-based with peat-based compost in about equal quantities. Never press the soil down hard with these plants. They all need feeding regularly when in full growth.

BELOPERONE (*Acanthaceae*)
MWT 10°C (50°F). Evergreen Mexican shrub with ornamental pink or yellowish bracts and insignificant white flowers. The shrimp plant is a popular house plant. It benefits from frequent re-potting and can grow to 90cm (3ft). Old plants can be cut back early in the year. Re-pot in spring in J.I.P.2 or peat-based compost. Water freely in summer and also feed. Cuttings of young shoots root readily with bottom heat. B. *guttata*, ultimately tall if not pruned.

BERGENIA (*Saxifragaceae*)

Cold. Hardy plants with handsome evergreen foliage and flowers very early in the year. The smaller varieties are worth considering for a shady unheated conservatory. Grow in soil-based compost grouped in an urn or in a ground bed. B.'Baby Doll', sugar pink: B. schmidtii, pale pink: B. stracheyi, pink, up to 30cm (1ft).

BILLBERGIA (*Bromeliaceae*)
MWT 7°C (45°F). Bromeliads from South America with curious flowers and long-lasting rosy bracts in winter or spring. B. nutans is the hardiest readily available bromeliad with greyish leaves. It can be allowed to grow into a clump in the pot. For culture see BROMELIADS. B. nutans, drooping sprays of yellowish-green flowers with blue margins and large rosy bracts, 30cm (1ft). B. x windii, similar with stiffer, wider leaves.

BLECHNUM see FERNS

BORONIA (*Rutaceae*)
MWT 4°C (40°F). Small evergreen shrub from Australia grown for the winter fragrance of their somewhat inconspicuous flowers. Grow in lime-free compost and keep moist but not sodden. Cuttings can be taken in summer. B. megastigma, brownish purple and yellow flowers, winter, 60cm (2ft).

BOUGAINVILLEA (*Nyctaginaceae*)
MWT 10°C (50°F). Deciduous climbing shrubs from South America with brilliantly coloured bracts. They must have sunlight to flower and need some restriction of the roots to flower well. In pots they should be trained in a spiral or loop. Grow in J.I.P.2 with a little added grit. Gradually reduce watering in October and keep almost dry from December to February when any necesssary pruning, potting and top-dressing is done. Feed with high potash fertiliser in summer. Cuttings are difficult. Young shoots with a heel of old wood can be tried in a propagator in spring. B. buttiana hybrids 'Mrs. Butt', rose-crimson; 'Brilliant', coppery orange; 'Temple Fire', brick red. B. glabra (Plate 24) and its hybrids are the most vigorous kinds with purple and magenta bracts. Some have variegated leaves.

BOUVARDIA (*Rubiaceae*)
MWT 10°C (50°F). Mexican plants with scented flowers over a long season. Useful for cutting. They need warm, moist conditions with shade from hot sun and are not readily available. 60cm (2ft).

BRACHYCOME (*Compositae*)
Cold. The Swan River daisy is a long-flowering half-hardy annual with a mass of daisy flowers. Sow in March or April and pot singly in J.I.P.2 or other compost. Support with twigs and keep well watered. B. iberidifolia, mauve, pink or white flowers, up to 60cm (2ft) under glass.

BRASSAIA (*Araliaceae*)
MWT 16°C (60°F). The Queensland umbrella tree is a popular evergreen house plant often called *Schefflera* and related to *Heptapleurum* which has smaller leaves also arranged like the spokes of a wheel. Grow in J.I.P.2 and re-pot annually in spring. Keep in bright light but not sun. This plant slowly grows large but can be restrained somewhat by not potting beyond a 20cm (8in) pot. Water less while resting from October to February but moderately otherwise. Feed every other week when growing actively. *B.actinophylla* (syn. *Schlefflera actinophylla*), ultimately a tree.

BROMELIADS
This large family of plants come from the American continent and are spread over a wide variety of climates and elevations from southern Argentina to the southern United States. They are often described as 'urn plants' or 'air plants' because many of them have a central vase which holds water and enables them to survive dry periods, while others appear to be living on air but are actually absorbing moisture from the atmosphere through scales on the surface of their leaves. In the wild most of them live attached to trees in tropical forests, or on rocks on hillsides and even on cacti. Bromeliads like orchids are a specialist interest but it is very much easier to provide conditions which satisfy them. They are relatively pest-free and many accept lower temperatures than orchids. However they do need some understanding to give lasting pleasure.

The most familiar bromeliads on sale in garden centres and supermarkets are colourful and effective but by no means the easiest to grow. They are mostly terrestrial kinds from the floor of tropical forests and need both atmospheric moisture and fairly high temperatures all the year. Do not be in a hurry to re-pot them as their roots are not extensive. The important thing is to keep their centres filled with water. For those who are not really interested in actually growing things the awkward aspect of bromeliads is that each rosette flowers only once and then gradually dies. New shoots emerge from the base of the old rosette but may not reach flowering size for two or three years. This slow time-scale has been somewhat eased by the discovery that flowering can be hastened by chemical treatment which is now available to the amateur. Enclosing the plant in a plastic bag together with a ripe apple is a homely alternative.

Most bromeliads grow in the form of a rosette of leaves with roots that are able to cling to the rough bark of a tree. In nature they grow where there is daily heavy dew, mist, or fairly frequent tropical rainfall. This we can emulate by regular spraying or dunking the plants. It is best to use rain water and an occasional weak foliar feed.

In the conservatory one wants to display these plants to best advantage. They can be fixed to pieces of wood, bark or artificial trees made of logs. In any case the roots need to be encased in some porous mixture of shredded bark and sphagnum moss and the bundle covered with a piece of bark and tied on. They will need regular spraying but little attention otherwise. One could make a mobile of the smaller *Tillandsias*. A visit to a specialist nursery is desirable before embarking on an elaborate arrangement.

BROWALLIA (*Solanaceae*)
MWT 10°C (50°F) for winter flowers. Easily raised from seed to flower for months. Tender perennial grown as an annual. Sow in March or April for autumn flowering and pot singly in 10cm (4in) pots. Grow in any ordinary compost and feed when buds are forming and occasionally thereafter. *B. speciosa major*, violet blue, to 60cm (2ft): *B*. 'Silver Bells', white; *B*. 'Sapphire,' dark blue with white eye; *B. viscosa* is more compact but less attractive, with bright blue flowers with white centres. There is also a white form.

BRUGMANSIA see DATURA

BRUNFELSIA (*Solanaceae*)
MWT 10°C (50°F). This is a shrub that can be grown in pots and can also flower all the year round if well suited. It likes heat and moisture and a rich soil-based compost. J.I.P.3 with an addition of leafmould or peat-based compost suits it well. Re-pot every other year. Prune lightly in spring. Cuttings need a high temperature to root. *B. pauciflora calycina* (*Plate 25*), violet fading gradually to white and known as 'yesterday today and tomorrow', ultimately 1.2m (4ft) but flowers at 30cm (1ft).

BRYOPHYLLUM see KALANCHOE

BUDDLEIA (*Loganiaceae*)
Vigorous shrubs from Asia to consider only in large conservatories. *B. colvillei* is a beautiful species with the largest individual flowers of the genus. They are violet-rose to crimson and appear in June. It is hardy in some sheltered gardens but worth growing under protection further north if it can be planted out. MWT 4°C (40°F). *B. asiatica* is evergreen and more tender but its scented spikes of white flowers are welcome in February. MWT 10°C (50°F). Grow in soil-based compost or neutral loam and prune back after flowering. *B. asiatica* is best in a large pot or tub and can be stood outside in summer. Both are ultimately tall.

BUSY LIZZIE see IMPATIENS

BUTTERFLY FLOWER see SCHIZANTHUS

BUTTERFLY PEA see CLITORIA

CACTI
If cacti are grown in a conservatory it will be for their ornamental and long-suffering qualities and not as a collection of rarities. Most globular and cylindrical cacti are best kept dry and cold from October until March. This enables them to be risked even in unheated structures against house walls in

sunny locations. They are commonly grown with a MWT 4°C (40°F) and are even happier with another 3°C (5°F). They can be grown at all temperatures that a conservatory is likely to be and in dry air where other plants would not flourish. Most of the cacti included in this book will flower regularly with reasonable care but do need sunshine and a cool winter rest to do so. A few spectacular cacti come from tropical areas and cannot survive winter cold.

There is great misunderstanding about the needs of ordinary cacti for water, root-room and feeding. In general J.I.P.2 with 1/4 by bulk additional sharp sand or grit will accommodate most cacti. They greatly benefit from being re-potted each year. Spring is the best time but it can be done when convenient between February and September. Remove what soil you can without damaging the roots and re-pot in one size larger.

It is not recommended but quite possible to grow mixed cacti and succulents in this soil mixture in bowls without a drainage hole. Put at least 2.5cm (1in) of gravel in the base and choose a bowl some 13cm (5in) deep. Be careful not to over-water and re-plant after a year. This is one of the few horticultural arrangements that can survive for a time above a radiator so long as there is full light. In warm conditions they will need occasional watering all through the year to avoid shrinking. It is, of course, safer to grow them in pans with drainage holes.

Cacti usually begin to grow in March and that is when watering must gradually start. In summer they can be watered like other plants although the soil should be a bit on the dry side before water is given. Cacti also benefit from feeding. Use the same sort of feed as for tomatoes but less often. Regular feeding is essential if they are grown in peat-based composts. In that case drying out may lead to problems as peat is more difficult to re-wet. With soil there is more margin of error in both watering and feeding. The globular and cylindrical cacti in this book will be found under APOROCACTUS, ASTROPHYTUM, CEREUS, CHAMAECEREUS, CLEISTOCACTUS, ECHINOCACTUS, ECHINOCEREUS, ECHINOPSIS, FEROCACTUS, GYMNOCALYCIUM, MAMMILLARIA, NOTOCACTUS and REBUTIA.

There are also members of the cactus family with flat, leaf-like stems and showy flowers that are epiphytes and do not grow in soil in nature. These have a different life-style and we call them Christmas cacti, Easter cacti, orchid cacti, etc. You will find these and their culture described under EPIPHYLLUM, RHIPSALIS, RIPSALIDOPSIS, and SCHLUMBERGERA.

The confused nomenclature of these plants does not matter to most of us who buy on sight what are in fact a variety of hybrids between different species that come from moist conditions in tropical forests and misty mountains in South America. They have been bred to produce the most desirable flowers on the hardiest plants. Whatever they are called they have epiphytic ancestors that grew in the debris in forked branches of trees in shady, warm, moist, but free-draining conditions. They do well with bromeliads, many of which shared their original habitats. Many people grow them very cool but they are clearly much happier above 10°C (50°F) and can be grown in room temperatures throughout the year. Ancient and healthy specimens of Christmas cacti often belong to people with no greenhouse or conservatory. Shade from summer sun is essential and so is watering throughout the year. A weak feed of a tomato fertilizer (high in potassium) can be given regularly except just after flowering when they like to be kept a bit drier. They do best in a peat-based mixture with the addition of sand or perlite to help aeration, at the rate of about 1/4 by bulk of the whole. Re-pot every year after flowering but only put into a larger pot when the existing one is full of roots. Cuttings are very easily rooted in summer and two or three can be grown together as one plant.

The larger jungle cacti often called orchid cacti are either much taller or more trailing than Christmas cacti and may have triangular stems. The upright ones will need support unless allowed to trail. The main flowering is usually in spring but some flower more than once. These plants like warmth and humidity and in dry conditions are helped by standing on trays of damp pebbles or artificial aggregate. Cuttings root easily in the warm months.

CALADIUM (*Araceae*)
MWT 16°C (60°F). Very handsome tuberous foliage plants from South America. They have elegant heart-shaped leaves splashed with pink, red or white (*Plate 26*). They are only happy above 18°C (65°F) when growing and need high humidity and shade. They must not be chilled even when dormant from October to March. Grow in peat-based compost with very good drainage. Re-pot yearly in spring when starting into growth at 21°C (70°F). The available plants are all hybrids and vary in size and in colouring.

CALAMONDIN see CITRUS

CALATHEA (*Marantaceae*)
MWT 16°C (60°F). A large family of stylish tropical foliage plants from South America sold as house plants and only suitable for warm shady places. They are closely related to and sometimes confused with MARANTA (which see). They are more difficult to grow and the ones listed here are upright herbaceous plants which will reach 60cm (2ft) or more in time. Their flowers are insignificant but the leaves are very beautifully marked. Grow in either peat-based compost or a half and half mixture with soil-based compost. Feed when growing actively and re-pot each year in late spring. C. *insignis* (rattlesnake plant), narrow leaves with snake-like markings, 30–60cm (1–2ft); C. *makoyana* (peacock plant) silvery leaves with elaborate darker designs and purplish undersides; C. *ornata* and its varieties have fine white lines on dark green leaves.

CALCEOLARIA (*Scrophulariaceae*)
MWT 7°C (45°F). The slipper flowers are of South American origin and have masses of pouched and speckled flowers for many weeks. The dwarf hybrids

are sold in flower as temporary pot plants. They are not difficult to raise from seed at various times of year as they need little heat. They will flower in 10cm (4in) pots of J.I.P.2 or similar compost. The shrubby kind with smaller yellow flowers used to be raised from cuttings but there are now F.1 hybrid seed strains. These will flower for many weeks in summer if sown early in the year. *C.* x *herbeohybrida* (*Plate 27*) has large and small varieties with flowers in a variety of speckled colours, from 23–60cm (9in–2ft); *C. integrifolia* (syn. *C. rugosa*) shrubby, with small yellow and reddish flowers and F.1 seed forms with yellow flowers, 30–60cm (1–2ft).

CALLISTEMON (*Myrtaceae*)
MWT 4°C (40°F). Slightly tender Australian evergreen shrubs with scarlet bottle-brush flowers. They like sun and fresh air. Grow in J.I.P.2. Water freely when growing. Keep nearly dry in winter. Trim back after flowering and re-pot every other year. Increase by cuttings in summer. *C. citrinus* 'Splendens'; *C. linearis; C. speciosus; C. violacea* (*Plate 28*). All have scarlet flowers in summer, ultimately 1.2–1.8m (4–6ft).

CAMELLIA (*Theaceae*)
Cold or preferably 7°C (45°F). Hardy evergreen shrubs with flowers in winter and early spring. They can be grown in pots and plunged outside in dappled shade from June to September. Use a lime-free compost and never allow the roots to dry. Feed during active growth. Re-pot every second or third year in March or April. They can be planted in the conservatory border but will grow large in time and need to be kept cool and airy in summer. *C. japonica* hybrids with single or double flowers, crimson to white; *C. reticulata*, rose; *C. sasanqua* varieties (more tender) white or pink.

CAMPANULA (*Campanulaceae*)
MWT 4°C (40°F). Perennial and biennial plants with attractive bell flowers for some weeks. *C. isophylla* is a trailer with blue or white flowers sold as a house plant and for hanging baskets in summer. *C. fragilis* is similar. They can both be raised from seed to flower the same year if sown early. *C. pyramidalis* (the chimney bellflower of Victorian times) is a nearly hardy plant to raise from seed to flower the following year. This is up to 1.5m (5ft) tall and discarded after flowering. It is sown in April and can be grown outdoors until potted up in autumn. They need a lot of water and feeding when the flower spikes appear. Grow them all in soil-based compost.

CANTUA (*Polemoniaceae*)
MWT 4°C (40°F). Small evergreen shrub from South America with cherry-red tubular flowers in spring. Pot in spring and re-pot or top-dress every year. Use J.I.P.2 or sandy loam and leafmould. Water generously while growing but keep only just moist in winter. Prune after flowering. Increase by cuttings of young shoots in spring in propagator. *C. buxifolia*, pink or red, April and May, 90cm–1.5m (3–5ft).

CAPE COWSLIP see LACHENALIA

CAPE HEATH see ERICA

CAPE PRIMROSE see STREPTOCARPUS

CAPSICUM (*Solanaceae*)
MWT 10°C (50°F). The ornamental peppers have brightly coloured fruits that last well. Some are sold as temporary pot plants for autumn and winter. They can be raised from seed sown in heat in spring. The smaller edible varieties can also be grown in pots and are quite decorative until eaten. Grow in soil-based compost. *C. annuum* (Christmas pepper) comes in various shapes and colours; edible sweet pepper hybrids such as 'Triton', scarlet fruits in autumn.

CAREX (*Cyperaceae*)
MWT 7°C (45°F). A graceful and undemanding variegated grass from Japan that is useful for contrast. It grows all the year and needs to be kept moist. The clumps can be divided in spring. Grow in J.I.P.2 or similar and feed occasionally in summer. *C. morrowii* 'Variegata', yellow striped leaves 30cm (1ft).

CARNATION (*Caryophyllacea*)
MWT 7°C (45°F). Perpetual-flowering carnations are not really suitable for a conservatory unless one has a special interest in them. They are not decorative as plants unless in perfect health and looked upon with indulgent affection. They need considerable care and a tall building and are grown for the cut flowers. There are a number of dwarf carnations in any good seed catalogue that can be grown as annuals and make reasonable pot plants. Grow in soil-based compost and discard after flowering, or take cuttings of the best. There are also recently introduced miniature carnations called 'Reve Pink' and 'Cardinal Red' which have a long flowering season and are sold either in flower or as young plants and do not exceed about 20cm (8in).

CASSIA (*Leguminosae*)
MWT 7° (45°F) but preferably higher. A genus of about 400 species, the majority from warm temperate and tropical regions of both hemispheres. *C. corymbosa* (*Plate 29*) is a fast-growing evergreen shrub from the Argentine with yellow flowers most of the year in a warm conservatory. Grow against a wall or in a large pot of J.I.P.2. Water freely in summer and keep rather dry in winter. Prune back in February. Renew by cuttings in heat or by seed. It flowers when small. *C. corymbosa*, yellow, late summer and autumn.

CELOSIA (*Amaranthaceae*)
MWT 10°C (50°F). Tender annuals with brilliantly coloured plumes beloved by municipal gardeners. Sow in 18°C (65°F) in spring. They need moist warmth and shade from summer sun under glass. Pot singly and flower in 13–15cm

(5–6in) pots of soil-based compost. C. *argentea* 'Cristata' (cockscomb) with fan-shaped crests, red or yellow, 30cm (1ft); C. *plumosa* in similar colours is the more attractive plume-like kind, 30–90cm (1–3ft).

CENTAUREA (*Compositae*)
Cold. Almost hardy silver-leaved sub-shrub from Corsica with ferny foliage that is useful in a ground bed where there is plenty of space but no heat. Raise from seed in spring. Alternatively it can be grown in a pot and trained as a standard with a bunch of ferny foliage on top. Improved forms have to be raised from cuttings. Cut back after flowering and use young shoots as cuttings in late summer. C. *gymnocarpa*, up to 60cm (2ft).

CEPHALOCEREUS (*Cactaceae*)
MWT 4°C (40°F). Tall columnar cacti from South America topped by long white hair in time. Useful for accent in flat arrangment. For cultivation see CACTI. C. *senilis* (old man cactus), ultimately tall.

CERATOSTIGMA (*Plumbaginaceae*)
MWT 4°C (40°F). Deciduous shrub from China with a succession of gentian blue flowers in late summer and autumn that is worth growing in a ground bed in a very cool conservatory. It is hardy in many parts of the country but often killed to the ground. It becomes a spreading bush but can be pruned hard in winter. C. *willmottianum*, blue, July to October, 90cm (3ft).

CEREUS (*Cactaceae*)
MWT 4°C (40°F). Tall columnar cacti from South America with blue-green fluted stems. Grow in J.I.P.2 with added grit and good drainage. Re-pot yearly in spring. Water freely in summer and keep quite dry from October to March in cold conditions. See also CACTI. C. *azureus*, C. *chalybaeus*, C. *jamacaru* and C. *peruvianus* are ones to look for. Ultimately through the roof.

CEROPEGIA (*Asclepiadaceae*)
MWT 13°C (55°F). C. *woodii* is a miniature tuberous-rooted succulent plant from Natal known as 'string of hearts'. It has hanging strings of tiny prettily marked heart-shaped leaves. A hand-lens is needed to appreciate the finer points of its flowers but it is very easily propagated from small tubers produced on the stems. When well grown it can make an interesting hanging pot and the stems can be several feet long. For cultivation see SUCCULENTS.

CESTRUM (*Solanaceae*)
MWT 7°C (45°F). Tall evergreen South American shrubs with clustered tubular flowers in summer. They are suitable for planting against a wall where there is room. C. x *newellii*, crimson, is the brightest. They are hardy against a south wall in Cornwall.

CHAMAECEREUS (*Cactaceae*)
MWT 4°C (40°F). The peanut cactus from the Argentine forms a rapidly

spreading cluster of roughly peanut-shaped shoots and has a succession of orange-scarlet flowers in early summer. Feed occasionally in summer with a tomato fertiliser to encourage flowering. Water normally in summer but dry gradually from the end of September and then keep quite dry until March unless kept in a higher temperature. *C. silvestrii*, orange-scarlet, prostrate. See also CACTI.

CHAMAEDOREA (*Palmae*)
MWT 13°C (55°F). Elegant small parlour palms with pinnate fronds that like warmth and shade from sun. For culture see PALMS. *C. elegans* (syn. *Collinia elegans*) is the most popular houseplant palm and grows quite slowly to about 90cm (3ft); *C. erumpens* (bamboo palm) has clustered narrow green stems and can eventually grow to 2.4m (8ft); *C. seifrizii* has larger fronds but only grows to about 1.2m (4ft). All are happy in room temperatures but can be accustomed to less warmth gradually.

CHAMAEROPS (*Palmae*)
MWT 4°C (40°F). These are the hardiest palms. They are fan palms and hardy in some parts of the country. *C. fortunei* (syn. *Trachycarpus fortunei*) ultimately tall; *C. humilis*, from Southern Europe, is the most suitable under glass and can be grown singly or as a cluster of growths, ultimately 1.8m (6ft). For culture see PALMS.

CHERRY PIE see HELIOTROPIUM

CHLOROPHYTUM (*Liliaceae*)
MWT 10°C (50°F). A tufted plant with variegated grassy foliage. This is one of the hardiest and most tolerant houseplants, originally from South Africa. It is particularly suitable for hanging baskets or pots and easily increased from rooted runners. It is happy in any compost if shaded from strong sunshine and kept moist. *C. comosum* 'Variegatum' is the form most often grown.

CHORIZEMA (*Leguminosae*)
MWT 7°C (45°F). Evergreen Australian shrubs which spread airily about and have small bright butterfly flowers in spring. Some are hardy in Cornwall. They like a dry atmosphere and can be tied to a trellis or trained to any shape. *C. cordatum* var. *splendens*, red, spring, and any others that can be found.

CHRYSANTHEMUM (*Compositae*)
MWT 4°C (40°F). The chrysanthemum is most often seen today as a year-round flowering pot plant grown with controlled day-length and dwarfing treatment. The conservatory owner may display chrysanthemums but is unlikely to grow them in the traditional way. They can be grown from rooted cuttings purchased in spring or even from seed but these are long drawn-out processes which are not ornamental until flowering time. The enthusiast will not be deterred but needs a book on this subject alone.

C. frutescens (the Paris daisy) is an easily grown plant sold for bedding in spring. It is useful in a conservatory as it is very easily raised from cuttings. If they are taken in autumn the plants will flower in April and May in a frost-free conservatory when they are very welcome. If a plant is then kept in the garden, cuttings can be taken when wanted. There is also a kind with double white flowers.

CINERARIA (*Compositae*)

MWT 7°C (45°F). The bright daisy-flowered plant universally known as cineraria is botanically a *Senecio*. It is mostly seen today as a dwarf temporary pot plant in full bloom in a wide range of eye-catching colours. Unfortunately both white fly and greenfly find it irresistible and a day's neglect in watering is never forgiven. They can be raised from seed in April to flower the following spring and should be shaded from direct sunlight. *C. cruenta* hybrids in a multitude of colours; *C. maritima* (syn. *Senecio maritima*), the silver foliage plant used in bedding, can be useful in the unheated conservatory to cool the hotter colours and can be over-wintered as rooted cuttings or grown from seed in spring. Soil-based compost is best.

CISSUS (*Vitaceae*)

MWT 10°C (50°F). Two evergreen climbing foliage plants of interest in the shady conservatory. *C. antarctica* (the kangaroo vine) and *C. rhombifolia* (formerly *Rhoicissus rhomboidea*) are familiar house plants that need shade and can be cut back when necessary. Grow in J.I.P.2 or similar compost and water sparingly in winter. *C. discolor* is a tropical climber that needs MWT 16°C (60°F) but has velvety leaves beautifully marked with silver and purple. It is a plant for warm moist conditions but water sparingly in winter when it may drop its leaves. Re-pot yearly in spring and feed every other week in the growing season. Increase by tip cuttings in spring in warmth.

CITRUS (*Rutaceae*)

MWT 10°C (50°F). Evergreen trees with scented flowers and colourful fruit for a sunny conservatory. Although ultimately trees, all the citrus fruits can be grown in pots. If edible fruit is wanted it is wise to buy a specially grafted plant. Home grown seed is chancey and can take many years to fruit. One can obtain trees that will not greatly exceed 1.2m (4ft) in pots. *C. limon* 'Meyer' (Meyer's lemon) is one of the best for a conservatory and also the calamondin orange, *C. mitis*. This is a small spineless bush and a favourite house plant which flowers and fruits almost continuously even when small. It comes from the Philippines and really needs MWT 13°C (55°F).

CLEISTOCACTUS (*Cactaceae*)

MWT 7°C (45°F). Columnar cactus with silver spines. Slow growing but in time forms a cluster of columns that look as if covered with silver fur. *C. strausii*, ultimately about 60cm (2ft). For culture see CACTI.

CLERODENDRUM (*Verbenaceae*)
MWT 10°C (50°F). An evergreen twining climber originally from West Africa is the only one of this tropical genus usually available. It has what appear to be white flowers with scarlet centres but the white part is the calyx of the flower. It is sold as a house plant but is better in a warm conservatory where it can climb to 3m (10ft). Grow in soil-based compost and re-pot each spring as fresh soil is needed even if not a bigger pot. Water very freely in summer and shade from summer sun. Water very sparingly in winter. This is not an easy plant but a handsome one. *C. thomsonae*, scarlet, summer; *C. ugandense*, blue butterfly flowers, both ultimately 3m (10ft), but flower at 60cm (2ft).

CLEYERA (*Theaceae*)
MWT 10°C (50°F). Slightly tender Japanese evergreen shrub with particularly attractively marked foliage. The glossy green leaves have grey-green marbling and cream edges that sometimes flush pink. Grow in a half and half mixture of peat and soil-based compost. Feed when growing actively. Re-pot yearly in spring until it reaches the size you want and then top-dress each spring. It can be plunged outdoors in light shade in summer. Increase by tip cuttings in warmth in spring. *C. japonica* 'Tricolor' is the one to ask for. This plant is sometimes confused with *Eureya japonica* to which it is closely related.

CLIANTHUS (*Leguminosae*)
MWT 10°C (50°F). Interesting but tricky shrubby plants from Australia and New Zealand with scarlet pea flowers. The Sturt desert pea, *C. formosus* (syn. *C. dampieri*)(*Plate 30*) is a difficult but fascinating plant with a weak root system, best grown in a hanging pot or basket. Professionals graft its seedlings on the seedling stocks of *Colutea arborescens* sown ten days sooner. This should be done before the first true leaves of *C. formosus* develop. *C. puniceus* known as lobster's claw is easier and more shrubby. It can also be grown from seed. It is semi-evergreen and grows tall in time. Cuttings need bottom heat.

CLITORIA (*Leguminosae*)
MWT 13°C (55°F). The butterfly pea is a twining climber from India with beautiful single blue pea flowers. It blooms in about four months from seed raised in warmth in spring. Grow in soil-based compost. *C. ternatea*, blue, summer, to 3.6m (12ft).

CLIVIA (*Amaryllidaceae*)
MWT 7°C (45°F). Handsome fleshy rooted plants from southern Africa with umbels of orange, apricot or yellow flowers in early spring in the sunny conservatory. Grow in J.I.P.2 or 3 or other rich soil-based compost and feed fortnightly from when the flower stalks are well-developed until the autumn. They are rested through the winter which means much less water but not complete dryness from October to February. They flower best when the pots are full of roots and need re-potting only about every three years when they

can be increased by division. Do not allow them to waste energy in setting seed. *C. miniata* *(Plate 31)* is charming and there are improved varieties including some with yellow flowers.

COBAEA *(Cobaeaceae)*
MWT 7°C (45°F). A rampant climber from Mexico to grow from seed and plant out where there is room for it to hang in long trails with its purple cup and saucer flowers. The seed must be fresh and germinated at 20°C (70°F) in February or March. Pot on in J.I.P.2. It can be increased by cuttings of firm side shoots in a propagator. Prune hard back in February. *C. scandens*, purple, and a white variety, 3–6m (10–20ft.)

COCOS *(Palmae)*
MWT 18°C (65°F). One sometimes sees a sprouting coconut in a garden centre and it is an interesting palm to grow in the early stages but a wholly tropical one. It has a slow-growing miniature relative, *C. weddeliana*, which is sold as a house plant. This has very finely divided feathery fronds and is sensitive to dry air. Grow in soil-based compost, feed regularly and shade from summer sun. *C. nucifera* (coconut palm) ultimately a tree; *C. weddeliana* (syn. *Syagarus weddelianus* and *Microcoelum weddelianum*) ultimately 90cm–1.2m (3–4ft).

CODIAEUM *(Euphorbiaceae)*
MWT 13°C (55°F). These evergreen tropical shrubs from South East Asia are known as crotons and need both warmth and some sunshine to maintain the varied and brilliant colouring of their leaves. Grow in J.I.P.2 and feed about twice a month from spring to autumn. Water freely while active and water less in winter but do not allow to dry. This is an easy plant in high temperatures. *C. variegatum pictum* has many forms with differently shaped leaves and a choice of splashed, spotted or marbled colour arrangements of red, pink and yellow on green.

COELOGYNE *(Orchidaceae)*
MWT 10°C (50°F). An orchid from Asia with pendulous white flowers in winter or early spring. It is always recommended for beginners as it is hard to kill. All the same it may live for years and not flower. Nevertheless mature plants produce many flowers and can be grown in a pan or a basket. For culture see ORCHIDS.

COLEUS *(Labiatae)*
MWT 10°C (50°F). The flame nettles are brightly coloured foliage plants from Java that are not normally worth preserving through the winter. One can raise attractive plants from a good strain of seed sown in heat early in the year. Cuttings root easily in the summer and rooted cuttings of named cultivars can be purchased from a specialist grower in spring. Pinch out the tips to prevent flowering. Warmth is essential for growth and shade from sun under glass. Any rich compost will suit them. *C. blumei* and its cultivars *(Plate 32)*.

COLQUHOUNIA (*Labiatae*)
MWT 13°C (55°F). Impressive evergreen soft-wooded shrub from the Himalayas now sold as a house plant. It is said to flower in about 18 months from seed. It is also easily raised from cuttings. *C. coccinea.*

COLUMNEA (*Gesneriaceae*)
MWT 16°C (60°F). Warm greenhouse trailing plants from tropical America that can flower almost continuously if their particular needs are met. They are epiphytic in nature and like a humid atmosphere and good light with shade from summer sun. Grow in half-pots or shallow baskets in a freely draining compost, either soil or peat-based with added perlite or sphagnum moss. Feed often with half strength tomato fertiliser in summer. Cuttings root easily in a propagator and the plants are best renewed each year with several planted together in a basket. They can trail for several feet. *C.* 'Alpha' is a yellow flowered modern hybrid and there are others with the more usual scarlet flowers. *C.* x *banksii* is an old favourite and strong growing; *C. gloriosa*, *C. microphylla* (Plate 33) and *C. rotundifolia* are all scarlet and trailing.

CORDYLINE (*Agavaceae*)
MWT 7°C (45°F). Evergreen foliage from South East Asia to Australasia that can be grown in conservatories when young. Grow in soil-based compost and re-pot every spring until they are in the largest practical pot or tub, then top-dress annually. Water freely during active growth but keep nearly dry in winter in cool conditions. Most can be increased by using sections of the stem as cuttings in spring or early summer. It is also possible to raise them from seed in heat. *C. australis* (known as the New Zealand cabbage tree) has sword-like leaves some 60cm (2ft) long. It ultimately becomes a tree that is hardy in southern coastal regions. There is a purple-leaved form, *C. a.* 'Atropurpurea'. *C. indivisa* is similar with wider leaves which soon take up a lot of space. Both are good tub plants to stand outside in summer. *C. terminalis* (formerly *Dracaena terminalis*) needs MWT 13°C (55°F). It has oval leaves 30cm (1ft) long. There are many forms with varying amounts of red, bronze and yellow suffusing the leaves. For cultivation see DRACAENA.

CORONILLA (*Leguminosae*)
MWT 4°C (40°F). Slightly tender evergreen shrubs from Southern Europe with clusters of small yellow pea flowers over a long period and glaucous pinnate leaves. Grow in J.I.P.2 or 3 and keep in a sunny and airy position. Cut back after flowering. Increase by cuttings of firm young shoots in late summer or raise from seed. *C. glauca*, yellow fragrant, and *C. g.* 'Variegata' with cream variegated leaves, 60–90cm (2–3ft).

CORREA (*Rutaceae*)
MWT 4°C (40°F). Small evergreen Australian shrub with scarlet tubular flowers. Sometimes called Australian fuchsia. Grow in J.I.P.3 or ericaceous

compost. Keep constantly moist but not in standing water. Trim after flowering. Increase by cuttings in July. The young plants need pinching to make them bushy. *C.* x *harrisii*, scarlet, 60–90cm (2–3ft).

COTYLEDON (*Crassulaceae*)
MWT 4°C (40°F). Succulent plants from southern Africa with very attractive pale grey foliage. *C. orbiculata* is shrubby with fleshy silver-white leaves with red margins. It comes in various forms and mature plants flower but are mainly grown for the leaves. *C. undulata* is a smaller plant with fascinating silver-grey leaves with wavy margins. Both are slow-growing. For cultivations see SUCCULENTS.

CRAPE MYRTLE see LAGERSTROEMIA

CRASSULA (*Crassulaceae*)
MWT 7°C (45°F). Easily grown succulent shrubs and herbs from Southern Africa for the sunny conservatory. Grow in J.I.P.2 or other soil-based compost with up to a third of added sharp sand or grit. Keep nearly dry from November to March but water freely otherwise. Increase by stem or leaf cuttings during the warmer months. *C. coccinea*, see ROCHEA; *C. falcata* (*Plate 34*), handsome blue-grey leaves and heads of scarlet flowers in summer; *C. arborescens* (syn. *C. argentea*), known as the money plant, is a slow-growing shrub, with pink or white flowers in winter after many years; *C. schmidtii* (syn. *C. impressa*), miniature plant with heads of tiny carmine flowers in winter.

CROCUS (*Iridaceae*)
Cold. Hardy bulbs which do not like warmth but are harbingers of spring in the unheated conservatory. The small early species and their cultivars are particularly rewarding. They can be grown in bowls, alpine pans or half pots and later planted in the garden. There are many to choose from in a good bulb catalogue. If kept watered after flowering they will do two years in the same pot. Of those most readily available in shops, *C. chrysanthus* varieties, *C. imperati* and *C. sieberi* will all give pleasure in January or early February.

CROSSANDRA (*Acanthaceae*)
MWT 18°C (65°F). Small shrub-like plants from India with attractive clusters of salmon-orange flowers over a long season. They prefer a moist atmosphere and a temperature of 20°C (70°F) but the variety 'Mona Walhed' is a popular house plant and the most tolerant. Grow in soil-based compost. Water moderately when growing and feed when active but keep nearly dry during the winter rest. Re-pot in a larger pot each spring. *C. infundibuliformis* (syn. *C. undulifolia*) (*Plate 35*) and particularly *C. i.* '*Mona Walhed*', salmon to orange, 30cm (1ft).

CRYPTANTHUS (*Bromeliaceae*)
MWT 13°C (55°F). These are small terrestrial bromeliads from South America, often known as 'earth stars'. They can be fixed to artifical trees with other

bromeliads or used for ground-cover in a warm slightly shaded position. They can be grown in peat or soil-based compost in small pots as there is little root. *C. bivittatus* with pinkish stripes on greenish brown leaves some 8cm (3in) long and the larger *C. zonatus* with green, white and brown zebra stripes are popular. See also BROMELIADS.

CUPHEA (*Lythraceae*)
MWT 7°C (45°F). The Mexican cigar flower is an intriguing tender perennial that can be raised from seed and has small scarlet grey-tipped flowers over a long period. Grow in soil or peat-based compost. *C. ignea* (syn. *C. platycentra*) about 30cm (1ft). Grow in any potting compost. *C. miniata*, pale vermilion, is a pleasant annual. 45cm (18in).

CUPRESSUS (*Pinaceae*)
Cold. Where there is no heat or just freedom from frost there are two slightly tender conifers worth considering. The Chinese weeping cypress (*C. funebris*) with graceful grey-green pendant branches and the Kashmir cypress (*C. cashmiriana*) are ornamental while young. Although forest trees they can spend a number of years in pots. Re-pot when necessary in spring when growth begins and use a soil-based compost with a little added leafmould or peat.

CYCAS (*Cycadaceae*)
MWT 10°C (50°F). Evergreen plants from Japan. They look like a cross between a palm and a fern but this is misleading. They are botanically primitive and extremely slow growing with a circle of stiff pinnate fronds. They develop a short trunk in time but this takes so long that mature specimens are very costly. However, it can be the ideal plant for a particular position and will remain so permanently. It is tolerant of full light and sun or some shade. Water moderately all the year and grow in soil-based compost to which a substantial amount of fine grit or perlite has been added. Re-pot only when it is obviously necessary. Keep in one position in relation to the light as the leaves do not readily adjust like other plants. This characterful plant can be grown from seed by the young and optimistic. *C. revoluta (Plate 36)* is the one most often seen.

CYCLAMEN (*Primulaceae*)
MWT 10°C (50°F). The long flowering season in winter makes this tuberous rooted plant a popular gift plant. It should flower for three months and will have been raised in a moist greenhouse at about 55°F. Trouble begins when it goes to market. Never buy from a pavement display in cold eather. Do not allow to dry or to stand in water. Inure cyclamen gradually to changes of temperature, both 17°C (45°F) and 18°C (65°F) are possible with care. John Innes composts suit them. The florist's cyclamen have been developed from *C. persicum* which is a charming conservatory plant with small scented flowers in March. In the frost-free conservatory other species available from bulb specialists are worth growing in alpine pans by those willing to care for them

when not in flower. C. *persicum*, white or pink with carmine centre; hybrids of many colours; the 'Rex' strain have leaves more heavily marked with silver; miniature strains are also attractive.

CYMBIDIUM (*Orchidaceae*)
MWT 7°C (45°F). The most adaptable orchids for growing in a conservatory. Flowers last for many weeks. They are evergreen and do not usually need a rest. Most cymbidium hybrids (*Plates 37* and 38) soon become large plants and need re-potting every other year. Flowering plants are six or seven years old and like ail orchids have to be understood or they will not flower again. Cymbidiums come in various sizes and the modern miniatures are the most attractive as pot plants. One very much needs to choose them in flower. For culture see ORCHIDS.

CYPERUS (*Cyperaceae*)
MWT 10°C (50°F). Tropical grasses known as umbrella sedges, which come in various sizes and are kept wet all the year round in pots of soil-based compost standing in a saucer of water. To increase, divide the clumps in spring. *C. alternifolius gracilis* is the smallest umbrella plant, to 45cm (18in); *C. diffusus*, up to 90cm (3ft); *C. papyrus* up to 2.4m (8ft) and needs a temperature 5°C (10°F) higher than the others.

CYPRIPEDIUM see PAPHIOPEDILUM

CYRTANTHUS (*Amaryllidaceae*)
MWT 4°C (40°F). These South African bulbs can only be bought from a bulb specialist. They are easy to grow six to a 13cm (5in) pot of J.I.P.2 planted in autumn and flowering in April. They increase rapidly and are good for cutting. They seem to do best if kept damp all the year. Re-pot only when very crowded. Hybrids such as 'Sunrise', apricot, April.

CYRTOMIUM (*Aspidiaceae*)
MWT 10°C (50°F). The holly fern is a popular house plant as it has shiny leathery fronds that survive dry air better than most ferns. For culture see FERNS. *C. falcatum* and particularly *C. f.* 'Rochfordii', 30–60cm (1–2ft).

CYTISUS (*Leguminosae*)
MWT 7°C (45°F). Yellow flowering brooms that are decorative for a few weeks in early spring. They are sold by florists as *Genista fragrans* but are *C. canariensis* from the Canary Islands or *C.* x *racemosus* (believed to be a related hybrid) with darker green leaves and deeper yellow flowers. Grow in J.I.P.2 or similar compost. Water freely from early spring until autumn but less in winter. Cut really hard back after flowering. They can stand outside from June to September. Cuttings can be rooted in spring or summer and will need pinching back to make bushy plants. Feed in spring and summer. They resent disturbance so feed rather than re-potting if possible.

A large lean-to conservatory used as a family living-room.

). A statue backed by a loquat (*Eriobotrya japonica*).

11. A statue and chairs among fuchsias in a large conservatory.

12. Carefully chosen plants for foliage effect make an effective composition.

3. Naturalistic and richly varied planting makes a convincing jungle view.

Simple staging accommodates a large number of different plants in a plantlover's conservatory.

15.   Striking contrasts of leaf and flower in a densely planted conservatory.

16. Abutilon hybrid.

17. *Acalypha hispida.*

18. *Aechmea fasciata.*

19. *Aloe ferox.*

20. *Ananas bracteatus* 'Striatus'.

21. *Aporocactus flagelliformis.*

22. *Begonia fuchsioides.*

23. *Begonia metallica.*

24. *Bougainvillea glabra.*

25. *Brunfelsia pauciflora calycina* and *Datura sanguinea.*

26. *Caladium* x *hortulanum.*

27. *Calceolaria* x *herbeohybrida.*

28. *Callistemon violacea.*

29. *Cassia corymbosa.*

30. *Clianthus formosus.*

31. *Clivia miniata.*

32. *Coleus blumei* 'Walter Turner'.

33. *Columnea microphylla.*

34. *Crassula falcata.*

35. *Crossandra infundibuliformis.*

36. *Cycas revoluta.*

37. *Cymbidium* hybrid.

38. *Cymbidium* hybrid.

39. *Datura mollis.*

DAFFODIL see NARCISSUS

DAPHNE *(Thymelaeaceae)*
Cold. Small hardy shrubs with very sweetly scented flowers in spring. Alpine enthusiasts grow them in pans and where there is no heat a single plant will scent the conservatory early in the year. Use a gritty soil-based compost with good drainage. They are best kept outside from June to November. *D. cneorum* and its varieties, evergreen, prostrate, rich rose pink to white, May; *D. collina*, evergreen, to 60cm (2ft), lilac, May; *D. mezereum*, deciduous, lilac purple, early spring; *D. odora* 'Aureo-marginata' is the variegated leaf form of the evergreen daphne that is a rare British native, valued for its delicious scent in mid-winter.

DATURA *(Solanaceae)*
MWT 7°C (45°F). Striking evergreen shrubby plants with very large trumpet flowers in summer. Only suitable for the large conservatory. They need to be grown in large pots or tubs or planted out. Some of them can reach 3.6m (12ft) in time. They need a rich soil-based compost and plenty of water in summer, so the drainage needs to be good. Keep just moist in winter. Pot and re-pot or top-dress in March. Prune fairly hard in October to control size. Cuttings of young shoots can be rooted in a temperature of 21°C (70°F) in spring or autumn. *D. cornigera* 'Knightii', double white; *D. mollis (Plate 39)*, cream; *D. sanguinea (Plate 25)*, orange red; *D. suaveolens* (angel's trumpet) *(Plate 40)*, white, fragrant.

DAVALLIA *(Davalliaceae)*
MWT 13° (55°F). Ferns, mainly from tropical Asia, with finely divided fronds that survive dry air surprisingly well. They have creeping hairy rhizomes and do well in shallow pans and hanging baskets. *D. bullata* (squirrel's foot fern); *D. canariensis* (hare's foot fern) is the hardiest; *D. fijiensis* (rabbit's foot fern) with larger fronds and more tender, up to 60cm (2ft). For culture see FERNS.

DENDROBIUM *(Orchidaceae)*
MWT 13°C (55°F). This extremely varied genus of orchids could be considered, if there is a real interest in growing things and the equipment for maintaining a really moist atmosphere every day. Many hybrids are available *(Plate 41)*. The choice must depend on personal preference and a specialist nursery should be consulted. For culture see ORCHIDS.

DICKSONIA *(Dicksoniaceae)*
MWT 7°C (45°F). The tree ferns come from Australia and New Zealand and are only of interest if there is space for a tree with a head of at least 3.6m (12ft) diameter in time. They take many years to form a trunk but can be transplanted when large and might be a feature in a large and shady conservatory, where they could grow in ground or in tubs. They must be well

watered all the year round. *D. antarctica* is the hardiest and most readily available. More tender tree ferns for higher temperatures are called *Cyathea* and *Alsophila* and may be hard to find.

DIEFFENBACHIA (*Araceae*)
MWT 16°C (60°F). Imposing foliage plants from tropical America known as 'dumb cane' because of the alarming effects of their very poisonous sap which can also cause great pain. They are sold as house plants but should be kept away from young children. They mostly grow on a single stem like a thick, soft bamboo with fleshy pale green leaves attractively marked with yellow, white or dark green. They become tall in time and to do well like a moist atmosphere and regular feeding. Keep in the best available light in winter but shade in summer. Grow in J.I.P.2. *D. picta* and its many varieties are the most frequently seen; *D.* x *bausei*, and *D. bowmannii* are some of the many others. The choice must be a personal one.

DIPLACUS see MIMULUS

DIPLADENIA (*Apocynaceae*)
MWT 16°C (60°F). Ornamental twining evergreen climbers from South America. Only one of the 40 species is readily available. *D. sanderi* 'Rosea' with lovely pink tubular flowers for several months in summer is sold as a flowering house plant in small pots. They can be planted out in a border in a warm conservatory or grown in a well-drained pot. Re-pot in J.I.P.2 every spring. They flower on the current year's growth which can be pruned away in the autumn, but do not reduce the main stem until the required height is reached.

DIZYGOTHECA (*Araliaceae*)
MWT 16°C (60°F). Elegant foliage plant from the New Hebrides. It has palmate leaves with narrow dark green leaflets backed with plum colour. This is an effective plant in warm shade and can stand poor light. Re-pot every other year in soil-based compost and water moderately all the year. *D. elegantissima*, slow-growing but ultimately tree-like.

DRACAENA (*Agavaceae*)
MWT 18°C (65°F). Most dracaenas come from the African tropics and need warmth and a moist atmosphere. *D. draco*, the 'dragon tree' of the Canary Islands, is the exception. A minimum winter temperature of 10°C (50°F) is adequate. These are foliage plants closely related to CORDYLINE (which also see). We grow them for their striking leaf-markings in white, yellow and occasionally red. I list some of the best known but there is a great choice. *D. deremensis* 'Bausei', and *D. d.* 'Warneckii are silvery green and white; *D. draco*, is an interesting oddity with plain green leaves, *D. fragrans* 'Massangeana' has large leaves with a vivid yellow central stipe; *D. godseffiana*, is a smaller branching plant with leaves spotted with cream; *D. marginata* is

palm-like with narrow leaves with red margins and also yellow stripes in *D. m. tricolor*; *D. sanderiana* is also slow-growing with small green and white leaves on cane-like stems. They can all grow several feet tall in time.

ECCREMOCARPUS (*Bignoniaceae*)
MWT 7°C (45°F). An evergreen Chilean climber that flowers the first year from seed. Although hardy in a warm corner this can be useful under glass in cooler places for its attractive foliage and racemes of flame-coloured tubular flowers. Sow in warmth in February or in late summer to over-winter in small pots. Cuttings will root in the autumn. Grow in soil-based compost or in a ground bed. *E. scaber*, orange-red, and *E. s.* 'Aureus', yellow, late summer, ultimately tall.

ECHEVERIA (*Crassulaceae*)
MWT 7°C (45°F). Indispensable easy succulent rosette plants from Mexico. Most have glaucous leaves and flower in spring. Grow in J.I.P.2 with additional grit or any well-drained compost. Re-root the tops of the plants when they become leggy and throw the rest away. Increase by seed, leaves or rosettes. There are hundreds to choose from. Water moderately all the year.They do well on automatic watering. Watch out for mealy bug, otherwise fool-proof. *E. affinis*, almost black leaves, dark red flowers; *E. agavoides*, pale green sculptured shape; *E. derenbergii*, blue-green red tipped leaves and plentiful orange and yellow flowers; *E. gibbiflora (Plate 42)*, larger grey-green leaves flushed red and winter flowers on tall stems, and *E. g.* 'Metallica' with a more gun-metal colouring; *E. glauca*, a hardy blue-grey one often used for bedding; *E. harmsii* (formerly *Oliveranthus elegans*) more upright with larger flowers; *E. pulidonis lutea (Plate 44)* yellow flowers; *E. Peacockii nummulosa (Plate 43)*, scarlet flowers; *E. setosa* with hairy green leaves; these are just some of the good ones. They mostly have flowers which are orange outside and yellow inside in late spring.

ECHINOCACTUS (*Cactaceae*)
MWT 4°C (40°F). Large globular cacti from Mexico that grow very slowly to an impressive size. For cultivation see CACTI. *E. grusonii*, strong cream spines; *E. ingens*, brown spines. They only flower after many years but the ribs and spines are highly decorative.

ECHINOCEREUS (*Cactaceae*)
MWT 4°C (40°F). Spiny cacti with showy flowers in summer. Most are frost-hardy if kept quite dry in winter. For cultivation see CACTI. *E. bristolii*, light purple flowers; *E. fendleri*, purplish violet; *E. pectinatus*, white spines, pink flowers; *E. pentalophus*, clusters of prostrate stems, violet flowers.

ECHINOPSIS (*Cactaceae*)
MWT 4°C (40°F). Globular cacti with unusally large pink or white flowers in

summer. For cultivation see CACTI. Hybrids of *E. eyriesii* and other species.

EPIDENDRUM (*Orchidaceae*)
MWT 13°C (55°F). Those who are going to grow epiphytic plants in moist conditions with some warmth can consider this vast group of orchids. They come from the same regions of South and Central America as the BROMELIADS but need more understanding. For culture see ORCHIDS.

EPIPHYLLUM (*Cactaceae*)
MWT 7°C (45°F). These are epiphytic cacti from South America. They have tall stems, few spines, and large showy flowers (*Plates 45* and *46*). They are not desert plants and most will need some support. Grow in a peat-based compost with one third by volume of coarse grit added to it. They appreciate tomato fertiliser when growing actively in summer. Re-pot in spring when really necessary. One can take cuttings in spring or summer. There are many hybrids to choose from, some tall, some trailing, Many flower more than once a year but late spring is the favourite time. *E. 'Ackermannii'* with many scarlet flowers is the best known and *E. 'Cooperi'* has white flowers that open at night. Otherwise it is a matter of personal choice from a specialist catalogue. The flowers can be 15cm (6in) across but the plants are not themselves beautiful.

ERANTHEMUM (*Acanthaceae*)
MWT 18°C (60°F). An Indian shrub with brilliant blue flowers in late autumn, winter and spring. Grow in very good light in a peat-based compost. Trim back after flowering and keep moist. Re-pot in spring or renew from cuttings which root easily in early summer. Feed regularly and water freely when growing strongly. *E. pulchellum* (syn. *E. nervosum*) (*Plate 47*), spikes of gentian blue flowers in late autumn and winter.

ERICA (*Ericaceae*)
MWT 7°C (45°F). The evergreen heathers we see in pots are known as Cape heaths and come from the mountains of southern Africa. They are temporary plants sold in bloom in winter and will last a great deal longer in the cool conservatory than in the home. They do not use much water but must never dry out. They need lime-free compost and prefer lime-free water. They are very much plants to enjoy and then throw away. *E. gracilis*, pink, and its white variety; *E. hyemalis*, long tubular flowers, pink with white tips, are the most often seen.

ERIOBOTRYA (*Rosaceae*)
Cold. The loquat is a small evergreen tree from Eastern Asia that has handsome leaves some 15–23cm (6–9in) long with a hairy surface when young (*Plate 10*). It will not fruit as a pot plant but is easily raised from seed and makes a reasonable foliage plant. Sow in spring and grow in any compost. *E.*

japonica, ultimately tall.

ERYTHRINA (*Leguminosae*)
MWT 7°C (45°F). A genus of some 30 species, usually trees or shrubs. *E. crista-galli* (coral tree) is a curious Brazilian shrub with a tuberous root rather like a dahlia and clusters of deep scarlet flowers in late summer. Grow in J.I.P.2 or 3 and keep dry and frost-free in winter. Soak in March or April and start into growth in warm conditions if possible. Re-pot yearly when growth has just started. They can be increased by cuttings taken with a heel of old wood in heat in spring. 1.5–1.8m (5–6ft).

EUCALYPTUS (*Myrtaceae*)
MWT 7°C (45°F). Evergreen trees from Australia with attractive glaucous and scented juvenile foliage. Gum trees are not a first choice for a conservatory but can be grown as annuals from seed raised in early spring. They quickly provide grey foliage and grow in any soil-based compost. All are fast-growing trees and like full sun. *E. citriodora* is lemon-scented; *E. gunnii* can be kept in pots for a year or two.

EUPHORBIA (*Euphorbiaceae*)
MWT 10°C (50°F). The vast family of the spurges is not one for the household where there are young children. All have sap which must be kept away from the eyes and some have sharp spines. The poinsettia, *E. pulcherrima*, is a favourite gift plant at Christmas and remains colourful for months. It has been dwarfed by chemical means and given artificial day length to time the flowering. If kept another year it will be much taller and is not often worth the bother. *E. fulgens* is another colourful and shrubby euphorbia for the warm and sunny conservatory while the plants known as 'crown of thorns' are small spiny shrubs with much smaller coloured bracts for much of the year. They are usually called *E. millii* and vary in size and the colour of the bracts. *E. tirucalli*, the 'milkbush' is quite a different plant with a mass of pencil-thin bright green stems. It grows eventually to tree-like proportions but is an easy and effective stand-alone oddity in warm sunny conditions. There are many tall-growing succulent euphorbias that look like cacti and any can be grown. *E. grandicornis* is a typical and handsome one. A small succulent plant of attractive shape with a crown of leaves and green flowers twice a year is *E. bupleurifolia*. This prefers shade in summer.

EUREYA see CLEYERA

EURYOPS (*Compositae*)
Cold. Small slightly tender evergreen shrubs from South Africa with attractive grey leaves which are useful for foliage effect in the unheated or frost-free conservatory. They also have yellow daisy flowers. Grow in a gritty soil-based compost in a sunny position and keep on the dry side in winter. Increase by

seed sown in spring or cuttings rooted in summer. *E. acraeus*, tiny silver shrublet, yellow, summer, to 30cm (1ft) *E. pectinatus*, grey leaves, yellow flowers, late spring, 60–90cm (2–3ft).

EXACUM (*Gentianaceae*)
MWT 10°C (50°F). Pretty scented flowering plant, originally from Socotra, with a long flowering season. They are sold in flower as temporary houseplants and appreciate a moist atmosphere and shade in summer. Seed sown in heat early in the year will flower in late summer but needs care. A mixture of equal quantities of soil and peat-based compost suits them. *E. affine*, masses of lilac-blue flowers, late summer and autumn.

FATSHEDERA (*Araliaceae*)
MWT 7°C (45°F). Useful evergreen foliage plant like a stiff ivy with larger leaves. It is a cross between ivy and fatsia. With support or against a light trellis it can be used to divide one area from another. One can grow them singly or several to a pot. Cuttings root easily. The variegated kind is slow-growing and needs stronger light. For cultivation see FATSIA. They are sold as house plants and will grow several feet tall in time. *F.* x *lizei* and *F.* x *l.* 'Variegata' with white markings.

FATSIA (*Araliaceae*)
MWT 7°C (45°F). Evergreen shrub from China that is hardy in much of the country and thrives in shade. It is also a popular house plant. Under protection its bright green glossy leaves become thinner and more delicate. It is easily raised from seed that is really fresh. Cuttings can be taken from shoots appearing at the base of the plant. These will need warmth and either a propagator or plastic bag. Grow in John Innes composts and re-pot infrequently if you want to keep them small. They can be cut back and will then branch. Water freely from May to September and only moderately in winter. The variegated forms are more tender and need stronger light. *F. japonica* and its variegated forms with white or cream markings; *F. j.* 'Moseri' is more yellow and compact.

FEIJOA (*Myrtaceae*)
MWT 40°C (40°F). Slightly tender evergreen shrub from Brazil. It has glossy leaves with white backs and white flowers with crimson stamens. Grow in soil-based compost or plant out against a wall. It can be grown from seed or layers. This plant is hardy in Cornwall but worth growing in the frost-free conservatory. *F. sellowiana*, white and crimson, autumn, ultimately a small tree with green edible fruit.

FERNS
The first thing to remember about ferns is that none of them can endure direct sunlight under glass. In a shady conservatory such as a lean-to facing north

ferns could be a major feature. In most conservatories they will complement other plants and decorate the shadier corners. The Victorians, who appreciated shade, made great use of ferns and had infinitely more to choose from than are in commerce today. Most of the ferns included in this book are sold as temporary house plants and have been chosen for their relative ease of growth and ability to withstand difficult conditions. To make a feature of ferns it is worth seeking out some of their very beautiful and less common relatives. The second requirement of ferns in pots is never to be allowed to dry out, while maintaining good drainage. A moist atmosphere is the aim although it is usually better to dampen the surroundings rather than the ferns themselves.

In nature ferns revel in leaf mould and the spongy soil of the forest floor. Many ferns are epiphytic and grow in the organic detritus to be found in fallen trees or amongst mossy rocks and other well-drained but moist positions. This means that the compost used for ferns needs to have a high percentage of organic material such as sphagnum peat or leaf-soil in its composition. One possibility is equal parts of sphagnum peat, leaf mould and coarse sand. Perlite can be substituted for the sand. Ferns in this compost will need regular feeding when in active growth. Ferns can also be grown in soil-based compost with the addition of leaf-soil or peat. A compost consisting of equal quantities of loam, leaf-mould, silver sand and very old dry cow manure with a little powdered charcoal used to be considered the 'dream ticket' for ferns but is unlikely to be attempted by many conservatory owners today.

Potting and re-potting is best done in spring. Never bury the centre of the plant. Many ferns do best in shallow pans and baskets if they are creeping species. Most ferns spread either by underground or surface rhizomes and need re-potting when they begin to climb out of the pot. A sharp knife is usually needed to divide them when they become too large.

When grown in warmth most ferns will remain active all the year but if the temperature falls many will become deciduous and rest until it is warmer. The adiantums, or maidenhair ferns, come from both tropical and temperate areas in widely separated continents. The crossing of ornamental species has made it difficult to define precisely the temperatures needed. Many ferns are able to adapt to widely differing temperatures if subjected to them gradually. When purchased most will probably come from a warm greenhouse with high humidity. The majority of ferns in this book would be happy at 13°C (55°F), many would survive 4°C (40°F) but 7°C (45°)F is a much safer minimum and 10°C (50°F) is better. As the temperature falls less water is needed and as it rises more atmospheric moisture is also desirable. See under ADIANTUM, ASPLENIUM, BLECHNUM, CYRTOMIUM, DAVALLIA, DICKSONIA, PELLAEA, PHYLLITIS, PLATYCERIUM, POLYPODIUM, POLYSTICHUM and PTERIS.

FEROCACTUS (*Cactaceae*)
MWT 10°C (50°F). Handsome strongly spined barrel cacti from the deserts of

North America. For culture see CACTI. *F. acanthodes*, *F. latispinus*, *F. wislizenii*, all ultimately large after 20 years!

FICUS (*Moraceae*)
MWT 13°C (55°F). The ubiquitous 'rubber plant' may find its way to the conservatory and also its more ornamental varieties. They are tough evergreen trees fairly tolerant of our harsh treatment in the home and readily available. Water sparingly in winter but plentifully in summer. The banyan tree, *F. benghalensis*, is another possibility and of a more branching habit. I prefer the strong design of the fiddle-leaf fig, *F. lyrata*, where there is room for it. Then there are the small leaved kinds, somewhat less tough but more graceful, *F. benjamina* and *F. buxifolia*. When there is little space the mistletoe fig, *F. deltoides*, is a tidy, slow-growing plant and produces tiny inedible figs. They appreciate shade and a moist atmosphere in summer. Use soil-based compost and re-pot only when clearly necessary.

FITTONIA (*Acanthaceae*)
MWT 16°C (60°F). Creeping evergreen foliage plants from Peru for warm shade. The green leaves are netted with red or white veins. Grow in peat-based compost or peaty soil. They are choice plants needing a moist atmosphere and care but can be used for ground-cover in larger containers. *F. argyroneura*, green finely netted with white and *F. a.* 'Nana', smaller and easier to grow; *F. verschaffeltii*, matt olive green leaves with red veins.

FREESIA (*Iridaceae*)
MWT 7°C (45°F). Extremely fragrant bulbous plants from South Africa. They need support and are ungainly pot plants but easily grown from seed or corms for their scent or for cutting. Sow from April to June for winter flowering. Pot corms in August. They can be plunged outdoors for six weeks until growth starts. Then keep near the glass and support with sticks and twine. There are many brilliantly coloured hybrids, usually sold mixed, to flower in spring, 30–60cm (1–2ft).

FUCHSIA (*Onagraceae*)
Cold to warm. Deciduous shrubs from South and Central America. Fuchsias are worthy of a place in any conservatory. They are valued for their long flowering season and ready response in size and shape to many styles of cultivation. Their only disadvantage is that they have a great attraction for white fly. There are thousands to choose from and the variety available in the best specialist nurseries is a revelation. A temperature of at least 7°C (45°F) is necessary for the continuous growth of fuchsias through the winter but they can be over-wintered in a state of rest under the staging or in a frost-proof shed with only enough water to prevent the root-ball from drying out. Cut hard back in February each year and re-pot in March. J.I.P.2 or 3 are suitable. Cuttings root extremely easily and are often rooted in late summer. These are

more difficult to get through the winter in adverse conditions than mature plants. Alternatively one can take cuttings from the new spring growth on old plants (preferably in warmth and early in the year). Whatever the method, fairly frequent renewal and careful training is rewarding. They grow fast as soon as the temperature rises and need ample water and rich compost to sustain flowering. Feed regularly every other week all through their active season. Grow in soil-based composts and be ever watchful for white-fly. *F. denticulata* (syn. *F. serratifolia*) is a species that can be encouraged to flower in late autumn. *F. arborescens* is an amazing plant more like a lilac than a fuchsia, with which to confound your friends; *F. fulgens* (if you can find it) has sage green hairy leaves and clusters of long light vermilion tubular flowers; *F. triphylla* was the original species to be named fuchsia and is more tender than most and mainly known through its hybrids which have distinctive matt and bronzy leaves. These are upright growers with orange scarlet to bright red flowers and need MWT 10°C (50°F). The vast number of hybrids of mixed origin vary in habit of growth, size and shape of flowers and slightly in hardiness. There are singles and doubles and small and large flowers as well as upright or pendulous growth. The choice must be a personal one. I particularly like 'Chequerboard', 'Citation', 'Lustre', 'Mrs. Lovell-Swisher' and 'Marinka' for growing in various ways, and 'Balkon and 'Cascade' for baskets.

FUNKIA see HOSTA

GARDENIA (*Rubiaceae*)
MWT 16°C (60°F). Small evergreen shrubs with very fragrant double or semi-double white flowers. Grow in bright light but shaded from sunlight. They are best grown in lime-free compost. If it is peat-based they will need regular feeding from March to September. They flower best when slightly pot-bound and will need a little pruning in spring to keep a neat shape. After flowering they can have flowering stems cut back. To induce flowering a steady temperature of 15–17°C (60–62°) is desirable. A damp atmosphere is necessary when the buds are forming. Winter flowering can be induced by the removal of flower buds in summer before they have had time to develop. *G. jasminoides* (syn. *G. florida*) double white and its various forms.

GAZANIA (*Compositae*)
Cold. Half-hardy daisy-flowered perennial from South Africa used in summer bedding and ornamental in shallow containers in sunny positions. They can be bought in spring and the best increased by cuttings in later summer. They can also be raised from seed. Grow in J.I.P.2 with good drainage. The flowers only open in sunlight. Those grown are all hybrids in shades of orange, buff and yellow and usually called *G. x splendens*.

GENISTA see CYTISUS

GERANIUM see PELARGONIUM

GERBERA (*Compositae*)
MWT 7°C (45°F). South African herbaceous plant with long lasting daisy flowers much valued for cutting. A new strain with the deplorable name of 'Happipot' is a real improvement for growing in pots. They flower sooner (four months) from seed and are more compact. The seed must be fresh. They are sold as flowering pot plants. Grow in John Innes composts with a little extra sand. There are other strains of G. *jamesonii* with single and double flowers in all the warm shades of pink, peach, buff, yellow, orange and scarlet. 25–46cm (10–18in). These latter kinds need quite large pots to flower well. A temperature above 10°C (50°F) is needed for reliable winter flowering.

GESNERIA see RECHSTEINERIA

GLORIOSA (*Liliaceae*)
MWT 10°C (50°F). Tendril climber from Africa and tropical Asia. This is an elegant and showy plant with red and yellow lily flowers in summer. The tuberous roots are planted in spring in J.I.P.2 or similar compost. Pot singly in 15cm (6in) pots. They are watered freely when growing and gradually dried off after flowering to be kept quite dry in winter but not below 10°C (50°F). All the same I have left them in a ground bed in a conservatory for several years without harm. They resent root disturbance and need a stake or string to climb. G. *rothschildiana*, crimson and yellow, summer; G. *superba*, orange-yellow and red. All kinds are very similar and climb from 90cm–1.8m (3–6ft).

GLOXINIA (*Gesneriaceae*)
MWT 10°C (50°F). Velvety-leaved tuberous plants with big bell flowers are correctly described as *Sinningia speciosa* hybrids but they are universally known as gloxinias. They are often bought in flower and last well in warm shaded conditions. They can also be grown from dormant tubers in the same manner as tuberous begonias. They like a growing temperature of 15°C (60°F). Feed with tomato fertiliser when the buds show. Raising them from seed needs a very early start and more skill. If kept for another year the tubers are stored dry in winter and not below 10°C (50°F). Re-pot in spring in a well-drained peat-based compost that can be kept constantly moist. A mixture of equal quantities of sphagnum peat, perlite and vermiculite is sometimes suggested but this will need regular feeding.

GOLDEN TRUMPET see ALLAMANDA

GRAPTOPETALUM (*Crassulaceae*)
MWT 7°C (45°F). Decorative succulent rosette plants from California and Mexico which are closely related to ECHEVERIA and require the same treatment. G. *pachyphyllum*, miniature bluish rosettes; G. *paraguayense*, greyish-white leaves.

GRAPTOVERIA (*Crassulaceae*)

MWT 7°C (45°F). Another succulent plant closely related to ECHEVERIA (which see). G. 'Dr.Huth's Pink' is an attractive pinky-grey rosette plant that branches freely.

GREVILLEA (*Proteaceae*)
MWT 7°C (45°F). A fern-leaved evergreen tree from Australia. This is a very useful foliage plant when young and can be grown in full sun or shade. Long used as a dot plant in bedding displays, it can remain in pots for several years. Hard pruning is possible but it is a forest tree and best with a single stem. A slightly acid compost is preferred but J.I.P.2 is acceptable. Water freely April to September and moderately in winter. G. *robusta*, ultimately tall. Easily raised from fresh seed.

GUERNSEY LILY see NERINE

GUM TREE see EUCALYPTUS

GYMNOCALYCIUM (*Cactaceae*)
MWT 4°C (40°F). Popular small globular cacti from South America that are free-flowering. Any of the many species and varieties can be grown and should be watered freely in summer. For culture see CACTI. G. *balianum*, red flowers; G. *horridispinum*, pink flowers; G. *mihanovichii*, yellow flowers, and G. *saglione*, pink flowers, are some to look out for.

GYNURA (*Compositae*)
MWT 13°C (55°F). Scandent shrubs from tropical East Africa with vivid purple velvety leaves. These are rapidly growing foliage plants that need sunshine and warm conditions. I think the evil-smelling orange flowers are best cut off. Grow in soil-based compost. They are easily renewed from cuttings and good in a hanging basket. G. *aurantiaca* is the more upright and G. *scandens* (syn. G. *sarmentosa*) more spreading. Both can be known as 'purple velvet plant' or 'purple passion vine' and will need pruning to keep compact.

HAEMANTHUS (*Amaryllidaceae*)
MWT 13°C (55°F). Interesting African bulbous plants for those who like the unusual. Grow in soil-based compost, with the nose of the bulb just showing and re-pot only occasionally immediately after flowering. H. *albiflos* has a flower like a white-bristled shaving brush and is more or less evergreen. It is a window-sill plant exchanged between friends more often than sold. The others are more spectacular and less reliable. H. *coccineus* is an extraordinary but impractical plant for a conservatory while H. *katharinae* and K. *multiflorus* are the ones to go for. They both produce handsome spherical heads of scarlet flowers in summer. The difficulty is to repeat the performance each year. They resent root disturbance and must be allowed to complete their growth after flowering. Then they can rest in our winter. They are sold as dry

bulbs but do not really have a wholly dormant season. If happy they improve each year.

HAWORTHIA (*Liliaceae*)

4°C (40°F). A large family of easily grown small succulents from Africa. They mostly form clusters of rosettes of dark green leaves with a pattern of white tubercles or warts. Grow in soil-based compost with added grit. Most grow more actively in winter and need some shade in summer. Do not allow them to dry out completely but water little when inactive. *H. limifolia*, dark green leaves, lines of white tubercles, 7.5cm (3in) rosettes: *H. margaritifera* (pearl plant), similar with slightly larger rosettes: *H. reinwardtii* has elongated rosettes some 15cm (6in) tall and comes in many varieties. These are amongst the most attractive.

HEDERA (*Araliaceae*)

Cold. The ivies are not to be despised as foliage or basket plants. In shade without heat they can be useful. *H. helix* varieties such as 'Gold Heart' are hardier than *H. canariensis variegata* 'Gloire de Marengo' which is a popular house plant. They do not need large pots or frequent re-potting and any soil-based compost should do.

HEDYCHIUM (*Zingiberaceae*)

MWT 7°C (45°F). Tall growing plants from Asia related to the cannas. They have handsome leaves and fragrant flowers and are suitable for growing in the ground or in tubs in large conservatories. *H. gardnerianum* is the hardiest and has a spike of yellow flowers with striking red filaments. They need plenty of water from April to October and can then be cut down and kept nearly dry in winter. *H. coronarium*, white, summer, 30cm–1.5m (3–5ft); *H. gardnerianum*, yellow, late summer, 90cm–1.5m (3–5ft).

HELICHRYSUM (*Compositae*)

MWT 7°C (45°F). Australian sub-shrub with graceful sprays of small heart-shaped felted silver leaves. A useful summer foliage plant in urns, baskets and borders that needs protection in winter. It has little root for its size and roots easily from cuttings in autumn or spring. Growth is rapid and flowers best cut off. Grow in J.I.P.2 with added sand. Useful to fill or conceal. *H. petiolatum*, silver leaves and varieties with yellowish and variegated leaves. Worth saving in unheated glass.

HELIOTROPIUM (*Boraginaceae*)

MWT 10°C (50°F). The 'cherry pie' of the Victorian conservatory is a soft-wooded shrub from Peru with very sweet-smelling mauve or purple flowers for much of the year. It can be grown as a half-hardy annual to flower when 30cm (12in) high or grown in the ground and trained up a pillar or a wall. It can also be kept in pots and cut back in the spring and grown as a standard and raised from cuttings. There used to be many cultivars but now it is mainly offered as seed.

HIBISCUS (*Malvaceae*)
MWT 13°C (55°F). Free-flowering tropical shrubs from China now readily available as house plants. Growth-retarding chemicals are used commercially to improve the shape of these ultimately large shrubs. They have showy flowers for several months. A position with some sunshine is needed. They really prefer a moist atmosphere and a temperature over 16°C (60°F) all the year. They flower at an early age and can be renewed by cuttings rooted in heat in spring or summer. Grow in soil or peat-based compost and feed regularly with a fertiliser rich in potash during active growth. Never allow them to dry out but keep only moist during winter. Prune hard back in early spring. *H. rosa-sinensis* has large scarlet flowers and there are hybrids in various shades of red and yellow. *H. r-s* 'Cooperi' has weaker growth and leaves with dark green, pink and white markings.

HIPPEASTRUM (*Amaryllidaceae*)
MWT 10°C (50°F). Handsome bulbous plants from South America, often wrongly called amaryllis. They have huge showy flowers in winter and spring. The plants usually grown are hybrids developed from a mixture of species and the time of flowering depends on the amount of heat. Prepared bulbs for Christmas flowering are also sold. They are more or less evergreen but sold as dry bulbs in winter. Opinions differ as to whether to dry them off for two or three months in late summer. Re-pot every other year in J.1.P.2, only half burying the bulb. Hybrids sold by colour, scarlet, pink, orange, white and white suffused with red, about 60cm (2ft). *H. aulicum*, scarlet, 45cm (18in) and *H. vittatum*, white with scarlet stripes, up to 90cm (3ft) are sometimes available. *H.* 'Gracilis', scarlet and smaller in all its parts and *H.* 'Scarlet Baby' are my favourites.

HOSTA (*Liliaceae*)
Cold. Fashionable hardy herbaceous flowering plants from eastern Asia, grown mainly for their handsome foliage. Hostas are often disfigured by slugs and snails in the garden. If potted up singly in a pot to fit the root, they will produce fresh leaves early under glass and can be plunged outside later or planted in the garden. The spikes of mauve or white flowers are secondary. The choice is purely one of taste. *H. fortunei* (syn. *Funkia sieboldii*) has glaucous ribbed leaves and many varieties with yellowish leaves or white edges to green leaves, 60cm (2ft); *H. lancifolia* is neater and also has varieties with white or yellow margins or centres to the leaves; *H. undulata* is smaller still and has varieties with white or cream leaf margins; *H. ventricosa* is another with variegated forms.

HOWEA (*Palmae*)

MWT 13°C (55°F). Favourite Victorian parlour palms better known as kentias. Single stemmed palms with graceful fronds and good resistence to a dry atmosphere. Grow in soil-based compost and pot firmly. Re-pot every second or third year until in largest pot you can handle. Then top-dress annually in spring and feed when in active growth. Water freely in summer and keep only just moist in winter when in cool conditions. Shade from summer sun. *H. belmoreana*, upright to around 2.4m (8ft). Forms a trunk in time: *H. forsteriana*, very similar but with more spreading growth. See also PALMS.

HOYA (*Asclepiadaceae*)
13°C (55°F). Evergreen climbers or trailers from tropical Asia and Australia. They have succulent leaves and umbels of waxy and sometimes scented flowers in summer. Good light with some sunlight is necessary for flowering. Hoyas do best in rough peaty soil with some charcoal and sand. Water freely in summer but very sparingly in winter. All but *H. bella* will need supporting in pots or training up walls. Do not remove flower stalks as more flowers appear from the same spot in subsequent years. Increase by layering or by cuttings in a warmed propagator. A well grown *H. bella* is the dream basket plant but more tender than the others. *H. australis*, climber, scented white flowers with red centres: *H. bella* prefers 16°C (60°F), upright at first and then arching over with white, crimson scented flowers at the tips of branches about 18in (45cm) long. It is best seen from below. *H. carnosa* is the hardiest and best known climber, ultimately to 6m (20ft). Scented white flowers with red centres. *H. c.* 'Variegata' is less vigorous with cream-edged leaves but all can be kept in pots for some years. *H.imperialis (Plate 48)*, dark purple flowers, ultimately tall.

HYACINTHUS (*Liliaceae*)
Cold. Hardy bulbs for colour and scent in winter. Hyacinths provide a solid splash of colour and a single one scents a whole conservatory. Without heat they will not flower very early but are worth having. They can be grown in any of the potting composts in pots or in bulb fibre in bowls without drainage. Half bury the bulbs and do not make the soil firm under them or they will lift. Keep moist, but not wet, and covered with black plastic in a cool cellar or shed. Otherwise plunge outdoors for six to eight weeks before exposing to the light. Dutch hyacinths come in several sizes, tending to become cheaper and more graceful as they become smaller. Those prepared for early forcing really do better in warmth. 'Cynthella' hyacinths are good for bowls and the 'multifloras' produce a clump of small flower spikes from a single bulb in early spring. They are all derived from *H. orientalis* from the Mediterranean area, including the small white 'Roman' hyacinths which can be forced into flower at Christmas in warmth.

HYDRANGEA (*Saxifragaceae*)
MWT 7°C (45°F). Hardy deciduous shrubs much used for forcing into flower in

pots. If bought in bud and kept watered the flowers will last for two months in cool shaded conditions. The earliness of flowering depends on the warmth available. For blue flowers the compost must be lime-free. One can also use a blueing compound. The plants used are all compact hybrids of H. *macrophylla* var. 'Hortensia', generally known as hortensias. The bun-shaped flower heads can be from red through pink to white or purple and every shade of blue to white depending on the variety and the acidity of the soil. It is not likely to be worth while for the conservatory owner to force hydrangeas but they can be planted outdoors where they will flower in August and September. Cuttings root easily enough but time and care are needed to produce good plants.

HYPOESTES (*Acanthaceae*)
MWT 16°C (60°F). A small foliage plant from Madagascar with dark green leaves prettily spotted with pink. H. *sanguinolenta* is sold as a houseplant mainly in an improved form with more pink colouring called 'Splash'. They need warmth and bright light although shielded from hot sun. Pinch out to induce bushyness. The flowers are insignificant and best removed. One can root cuttings in water of the best plants. They can also be raised from seed in warmth. Grow in soil-based compost and discard when they become straggly.

IMANTOPHYLLUM see CLIVIA

IMPATIENS (*Balsaminaceae*)
MWT 13°C (55°F). Tender continuously flowering annuals and perennials from tropical areas of Africa, India and New Guinea. They are mostly hybrids of I. *walleriana* with improved shape or colouring. Many can be raised from seed, and cuttings will root in a glass of water. They are known as 'busy Lizzies' and used for bedding in summer where they are excellent in shade. Those known as New Guinea hybrids are a more recent introduction and make large plants. Many have leaves with yellow or cream variegation. All are rather difficult to get through the winter and need frequent renewal from seed or cuttings. The flowers are of every shade of red, pink, orange, magenta and white. One can have plants from 15cm (6in) to 60–90cm (2–3ft) in height.

IOCHROMA (*Solanaceae*)
MWT 7°C (45°F). Rarely seen but attractive evergreen shrubs from South America with clusters of tubular flowers in summer and autumn. Treat as CESTRUM to which they are related. I. *grandiflora*, rich purple, late summer, climber; I. *tubulosa*, deep blue, late summer, about 90cm (3ft).

IPOMOEA (*Convolvulaceae*)
MWT 10°C (50°F). The morning glory and the blue dawn flower are both tropical climbers with sensational blue trumpet flowers in summer. I. *rubro-caerulea* (morning glory) (*Plate 49*) is an annual to grow from seed in warmth in April. Soak the seed, sow in pots, and do not disturb the roots when

re-potting. Grow in soil-based compost in a sunny position. *I. learii* (syn. *Pharbitis learii*) is a perennial for growing in the ground in a large conservatory. It is extremely vigorous and evergreen but becomes deciduous at low temperatures. Both produce a succession of short-lived flowers and quite a lot of debris to sweep up.

IRESINE (*Amaranthaceae*)
MWT 10°C (50°F). Tender herbaceous foliage plants from tropical America with coloured leaves used in bedding and for pots. They need good light and some sunlight. Grow in soil-based compost and re-pot when the roots show on the surface of the soil. Water freely except during winter rest when they should be barely moist. Renew frequently from cuttings which can be rooted in water in spring. This plant is not beautiful. *I. herbstii*, beetroot-red foliage; *I. h.* 'Aureoreticulata', similar but mottled with yellow; both up to 60cm (2ft).

IRIS (*Iridaceae*)
Cold. The early miniature hardy bulbous irises are a welcome source of colour and scent in the unheated conservatory. Pot in September or October about five to a 13cm (5in) pot or pan in J.I.P.2 or other soil-based compost and keep cool and just moist until growth is seen. They can be kept in a cold frame until just before flowering, or even plunged outside. After flowering plant out in the garden or water until the leaves fade. Then keep quite dry until autumn planting time. *I. danfordiae* tends to break up into small bulblets but the others can be re-potted for another season. *I. danfordiae*, golden yellow, January, 13cm (5in); *I. histrioides major*, ultramarine, January, 10cm (4in); *I. reticulata*, purple-blue, fragrant and its named varieties in shades of purple and blue.

IVY see HEDERA

IXORA (*Rubiaceae*)
MWT 16°C (60°F). Handsome slow-growing evergreen shrub from tropical Asia with clusters of scarlet flowers at the tips of the branches. They are now sold as house plants but need both good light and a humid atmosphere to do well. A happy plant should bloom for several months in summer. Grow in J.I.P.3 or other rich soil-based compost. Water freely in summer and shade from strong sun. Keep much drier from October to February when it can be re-potted and pruned back if necessary, although flowering shoots will be lost. *I. coccinea*, scarlet, and its varieties in shades of red, orange and yellow. up to 90cm (3ft).

JACARANDA (*Bignoniaceae*)
MWT 10°C (50°F). Brazilian flowering tree with bright green ferny foliage and blue flowers when mature. It is not very likely to flower in the conservatory but is easily raised from seed in real warmth in spring. It can remain in pots of soil-based compost for some years and bears cutting back. Cuttings of side shoots can be rooted in warmth in summer. *J. mimosifolia* (syn. *J. ovalifolia*),

lavender blue, ultimately a tree.

JACOBEAN LILY see SPREKELIA

JACOBINIA (*Acanthaceae*)
MWT 10°C (50°F). Shrubby plants from tropical America with handsome heads of pink flowers at the tips of the branches. Jacobinias, like fuchsias, are best renewed from cuttings quite often. Cut back old plants severely and give little water in winter. Grow in J.I.P.2 or similar compost and water freely in summer when they will need shading. *J. carnea* (syn. *Justicia carnea*) pink, late summer, ultimately 1.5m (5ft). This is the hardiest and even it prefers a higher temperature. *J. pauciflora* (syn. *Libonia floribunda*) is a much smaller plant with downy leaves and scarlet and yellow flowers but needs at least MWT 13°C (55°F). It flowers in winter and early spring, 30–60cm (1–2ft).

JASMINUM (*Oleaceae*)
Cold to warm. Evergreen twining and scandent shrubs with sweet-scented flowers. One can have jasmines at any temperature. *J. officinale* (common jasmine) is hardy and *J. mesnyi* almost hardy. Perhaps the favourite is *J. polyanthum* now sold in flower in pots. It is an easy and very fast-growing climber with clusters of pink-backed white flowers in late winter and early spring. It is suitable for any temperature above 4°C (40°F). *J. azoricum* needs a warm conservatory. All can be grown in J.I.P.2 or ordinary loam soil in a border. They need good light and do not flower in shade. They can all be grown in pots if re-potted yearly and fed while active. When grown in the ground they tend to be rampant. *J. azoricum*, white, summer and autumn; *J. mesnyi* (syn. *J. primulinum*), yellow, scentless, early spring; *J. officinale*, white, summer and autumn; *J. polyanthum*, white with pink buds, late winter and spring.

JATROPHA (*Euphorbiaceae*)
MWT 10°C (50°F). Caudiform plant from Central America grown as a curiosity. It looks like a large bulb with succulent leaves and scarlet flowers on top. It has to have a dry rest in winter when the leaves have fallen. Grow in J.I.P.2 with added sand in a sunny position and water normally in summer. *J. podagrica* is sold in garden centres; others may be found in cactus nurseries.

JUBAEA see PALMS

JUSTICIA see JACOBINIA

KALANCHOE (*Crassulaceae*)
MWT 10°C (50°F). An interesting succulent family from tropical Africa with two foliage and two flowering plants for a conservatory. *K. blossfeldiana* flowers naturally in spring and summer but commercial growers can induce flowering all the year with daylight manipulation. The modern hybrids need

bright light and plenty of water. They are mostly scarlet but also yellow and pink. *K. pumila (Plate 50)* is a small, spreading, silver-leaved plant with pink flowers in spring. It is good as an edging to a display bench or bed or in a hanging basket. *K. beharensis* is an ultimately large but slow-growing foliage plant with big velvety leaves on a single stem. *K. tomentosa* (panda plant) has small leaves with a silver plush surface and dark brown tips, ultimately 60cm (2ft). Grow in J.I.P.2 with added grit and re-pot yearly in spring. Keep rather dry in winter but water freely otherwise. All are easily increased from tip cuttings.

KENTIA see HOWEA

KLEINIA see SENECIO

LACHENALIA (*Liliaceae*)
MWT 7°C (45°F). South African bulbous plants with a very long flowering season in winter and early spring. Pot in August just burying the bulbs in J.I.P.2 or similar soil-based compost. Put about five to a 13cm (5in) pot. Water moderately until growing strongly and keep in the best light available. Water freely until foliage begins to die down. Then dry off gradually and leave quite dry on a shelf in the sun until re-potting in early August. *L. aloides* (syn. *L. tricolor*) has hybrids with deep yellow flowers sometimes tipped with green or red. *L. bulbifera* (better known as *L. pendula*), is coral red and flowers in December. All are about 23cm (9in). They will survive with only freedom from frost.

LAGERSTROEMIA (*Lythraceae*)
MWT 7°C (45°F). Evergreen flowering shrubs from Asia with frilly flowers in late summer. They are known as crape myrtle and popular in countries with hotter summers than ours. There is a miniature strain to grow from seed which flowers the first year but otherwise they are shrubs to train against a warm wall of the conservatory. *L. indica (Plate 51)*, pink, crimson, purple and white, ultimately a tree; also a miniature form to grow in a 15cm (6in) pot, up to 45cm (18in).

LANTANA (*Verbenaceae*)
MWT 7°C (45°F). Evergreen shrubs from the West Indies flowering the first year from seed. The better hybrids are increased by cuttings which root easily in August. Their merit is a long season of flowering and they will grow in any ordinary soil. *L. camara* hybrids with flowers like verbena in various colours mostly orange, yellow and pink, ultimately tall but can be hard pruned. A dangerous weed in warm countries.

LAPAGERIA (*Liliaceae*)
MWT 4°C (40°F). An evergreen twining climber of great distinction and beauty. It is the national flower of Chile and was named after the Empress Josephine (de la Pagerie). It needs freedom from frost, shade in summer and a lime-free soil. If

grown in a container 3 parts by bulk of fibrous peat, 1 part loam, 1/2 part sharp sand and some charcoal would be ideal. Water freely from April to September but keep only just moist in winter. Increase by layering. *L. rosea*, rose-crimson fleshy bell-flowers, late summer and autumn and *L. r.* var. superba. There are improved forms in various shades of crimson, pink and white (*Plate 52*).

LASIANDRA see TIBOUCHINA

LEMON see CITRUS

LEMON-SCENTED VERBENA see LIPPIA

LEPTOSPERMUM (*Myrtaceae*)
MWT 4°C (40°F). Evergreen shrubs from New Zealand that are almost hardy. They have minute dark green leaves and a mass of small flowers in early summer. Grow in neutral or acid soil. *L. scoparium* (manuka or tea tree of New Zealand) is easily raised from seed and has white flowers. The hybrids with single or double flowers in various shades from crimson to white can be increased by cuttings in May. From 60cm (2ft) upwards.

LEUCADENDRON (*Proteaceae*)
MWT 4°C (40°F). The silver tree of Table Mountain is an unusual foliage plant to raise from seed. The evergreen leaves have a silky sheen. Germination may be slow. Grow in J.I.P.2 or similar compost. *L. argenteum*, ultimately a tree.

LIBONIA see JACOBINIA

LILIUM (*Liliaceae*)
Cold to warm. Most hardy lilies are handsome in pots or tubs and particularly welcome where they do not do well in the garden. The modern hybrids are increasingly sold in flower but are not difficult to grow in pots. Lilies are potted directly into their flowering pots, either singly in a 15 or 18cm (6 or 7in) pot or grouped together in a larger container. The soil needs to be lime-free for *L. auratum*, *L. brownii* and *L. japonicum*. Otherwise one part of peat and one part of sharp sand added to every two parts of J.I.P.2 makes a suitable compost. Pot them up as soon as they are available in autumn. *L. candidum* and *L. testaceum* should be planted in August. Lilies are not really dry bulbs and are best purchased from a lily specialist if one is taking a serious interest in them. The stem-rooting lilies need to be planted deep in the pot and only just covered, so that there is room for top-dressing later. They should be kept just moist and protected from frost. They are best plunged in a cold frame or in a cool cellar until growth shows. Then bring them into the conservatory and watch out for greenfly. Give more water as the roots develop and feed regularly when the pots are full of roots. After flowering allow them to die down naturally. They can stand outside but should never become totally dry. If they are not going to be planted out in the garden bring them in before frost and

re-pot in fresh soil in autumn. Always take care not to injure the live roots. Increase by removing offsets in autumn. Favourite lilies for growing in pots are: *L. auratum* (golden-rayed lily of Japan), white with yellow markings, stem-rooting, and its many varieties, July and August, 90cm–2.4m (3–8ft); *L. longiflorum*, white, fragrant, stem-rooting, July, 90cm–1.8m (3–6ft); *L. speciosum*, white suffused and spotted with claret red, also its many named forms with varied colour, flowering time depends on warmth, 60cm–1.2m (2–4ft). The modern hybrid strains are a good choice for healthiness and ease of growth.

LIMONIUM (*Plumbaginaceae*)
Cold. There is one form of annual statice that is quite effective in pots. It has lavender-pink spires of bloom in summer which are sometimes dried for flower-arrangement. Sow in March or April and later pot singly in J.I.P.2 or any potting compost. They need plenty of water when growing strongly. *L. suworowii*, lavender-rose, 45cm (18in).

LIPPIA (*Verbenaceae*)
Cold. Slightly tender deciduous shrub from Chile valued for the glorious scent of its crushed leaves. It is naturally an ungainly bush and has to be kept to the required shape and size by pruning in winter to within an inch of the previous year's growth. Grow in soil-based compost. Increase by cuttings taken with a heel of older wood in early summer, preferably in a propagating frame. *L. citriodora* (syn. *Aloysia citriodora*) better known as lemon-scented verbena.

LIVISTONA see PALMS '

LOBELIA (*Campanulaceae*)
MWT 4°C (40°F). Half-hardy bedding plant valued for its long flowering season and clear blue colour. It is actually a perennial from South Africa and not to be despised in the cool or cold conservatory. It survives the winter if frost is excluded and flowers to November but is easily raised from seed in early spring. Transplant small clusters of seedlings as one plant. The light blue and white forms blend with anything. They will grow in any potting compost. *L. erinus*, compact and trailing varieties, light blue, dark blue, blue with white centres and various shades of crimson to white. 15cm (6in).

LOBIVIA (*Cactaceae*)
MWT 4°C (40°F). Miniature globular cacti from Bolivia, of which its name is an anagram. They are easy and free-flowering. Any can be grown. The flowers are mostly bright red or yellow. For culture see CACTI.

LOBSTER'S CLAW see CLIANTHUS

LOTUS (*Leguminosae*)
MWT 10°C (50°F). Silver-leaved trailing perennial from the Canary Islands with

clusters of scarlet pea flowers in May. It likes sun and is a tricky plant to please. It is not often seen in commerce. Grow in J.I.P.2 with a little charcoal or add additional leafmould and sand. It looks well hanging from a basket which really needs three plants, but it may be easier to watch over it in a pot. Water carefully in summer and keep only just moist in autumn and winter. Cuttings can be rooted in warmth in late spring. *L. Bertholetii* (syn. *L. peliorrynchus*), scarlet, early summer.

LUCULIA (*Rubiaceae*)
MWT 7°C (45°F). Deciduous shrub from the temperate parts of East Asia with attractive foliage and flowers. They grow best planted out in a border but the rooting area should be restricted as with a fig tree. If confined to a pot it will be more compact and flower quite well in a large pot. Grow in soil-based compost. In the border it likes sandy loam and peat. Water very freely in summer but keep barely moist during the first three months of the year. Prune back after flowering. The large heads of fragrant pink flowers are born on the current year's growth. Cuttings can be rooted in summer. Seeds take two or three years to flower. *L. gratissima*, pink, late autumn, ultimately tall.

MAMMILLARIA (*Cactaceae*)
MWT 4°C (40°F). This is a huge family of mostly bun-shaped cacti. Those with the most attractive spine formations and brightest flowers earn a place in the conservatory. In time they form clusters and many have red fruits after the flowers. They may be grown singly in small pots and do best if re-potted yearly in spring. Another idea is to group them in a bowl with other succulents or in platoons of identical plants in neat rows which can form an effective decoration. Grow in 3 parts J.I.P.2 to 1 part grit or sharp sand. Water freely in summer, less in September and keep dry from October to March. *M. hahniana* and *M. zeilmanniana* are two free-flowering ones with reddish-purple flowers. See also CACTI.

MANDEVILLA (*Apocynaceae*)
MWT 7°C (45°F). A deciduous climber from South America suitable for the larger conservatory. It is known as Chilean jasmine and has fragrant creamy-white flowers in summer. It should be planted out and trained up to the rafters where there is height and sunshine. It does not do very well in pots or in stuffy conditions. Increase by cuttings of firm side-shoots in a propagating frame in spring, or grow from seed. Cut back superfluous sideshoots in winter, leaving the main stem intact. A well-drained peaty soil with plenty of sharp sand suits it best. *M. suaveolens*, white, summer, up to 6m (20ft).

MANUKA see LEPTOSPERMUM

MARANTA (*Marantaceae*)
MWT 18°C (65°F). These low-growing foliage plants are valued for the

attractive markings on their leaves. They are known as prayer plants because they fold their leaves as in prayer at night. Grow in a peat-based compost in shade. They are easier to grow than the closely related *Calatheas* and although they may withstand a temperature as low as 10°C (50°F) in winter they are not worth growing in cool conditions. *M. leuconeura* in its several forms is grown as a house plant. *M. l. erythroneura*, red and light green featherings; *M. l. kerchoviana*, pale green leaves with brownish rabbit's foot markings are the most popular.

MARGUERITE see CHRYSANTHEMUM

MAURANDIA (*Scrophulariaceae*)
MWT 7°C (45°F). Perennial climbing or trailing plants from Mexico with trumpet flowers. They are usually grown as annuals and will bloom in 13cm (5in) pots. Sow in warmth in spring and give plenty of water while growing and feed when buds show. Keep almost dry if kept through the winter. Cuttings can be taken in summer. *M. barclaiana*, rose or purple, is the favourite; *M. erubescens*, handsome maroon-pink climber; *M. scandens* (syn. *M. lophospermum*), smaller lavender to reddish-purple flowers and neat leaves.

MEDINILLA (*Melastomataceae*)
MWT 18°C (65°F). This magnificent tropical epiphytic plant from the Philippines can grow large and its flower stalks hang downwards. The place for it is a carefully tended large hanging basket in a large warm conservatory. It seems to need a dormant period in winter to develop flower buds but even then the temperature should not fall below 16°C (60°F). *M. magnifica*, with clusters of drooping pink flowers, up to 1.2m (4ft). If it becomes too large for a basket a tall pot or pedestal will be needed. Prune back all growth immediately after flowering and grow in bromeliad compost. *M. magnifica (Plate 53)*, pink bracts and flowers, up to 1.2m (4ft).

MELALEUCA (*Myrtaceae*)
MWT 4°C (40°F). Evergreen shrub from Australia with scarlet bottle-brush flowers. It is related to callistemons but has smaller leaves and requires similar treatment. *M. fulgens*, flowers in June, ultimately tall.

MELIANTHUS (*Melianthaceae*)
Cold. Slightly tender semi-woody evergreen foliage shrub from South Africa that can be grown in the ground in a large conservatory. It has large very decorative glaucous pinnate leaves which smell of boiled milk if brushed against. It dies back to the ground outdoors but can be trained up to the roof in shelter. It can be raised from seed. *M. major*, brownish red flowers in summer.

MIKANIA see SENECIO

MIMOSA see ACACIA

MIMULUS (*Scrophulariaceae*)
MWT 4°C (40°F). Small shrubby evergreen from California with a succession of trumpet flowers in summer and autumn. This is not an exciting plant but the orange colour may be wanted and it is a manageable size. Pot in spring in J.I.P.2 or soil-less compost and re-pot each year. Water well in summer and train up a cane. Prune in early spring to keep in shape. *M. glutinosus* (syn. *Diplacus glutinosus*) (*Plate 54*), apricot, up to 1.5m (5ft).

MONSTERA (*Araceae*)
MWT 10°C (50°F). Evergreen climbing plant from Mexico popularly known as the Swiss cheese plant. They have attractive slit leaves but tend to grow too large indoors. They prefer a soil-based compost with extra leaf mould and should be re-potted in spring. Shade from summer sun and do not over-water. *M. deliciosa* (sometimes sold as *Philodendron pertusum*) and its variegated variety with cream-splashed leaves need a firm support.

MORNING GLORY see IPOMOEA

MUSA (*Musaceae*)
MWT 7°C (45°F). The banana family are tropical plants of tree-like growth which can be used for foliage effect while young. Well-soaked seeds sown in heat will grow rapidly in warm moist conditions. They can also be raised from suckers in a temperature of at least 16°C (60°F). Feed and water freely. Shade from full summer sun under glass. *M. basjoo, M. cavendishii, M. coccinea, M. ensete* and *M. paradisiaca* are sometimes offered. All are ultimately tall but unlikely to be kept through the winter.

MYRTUS (*Myrtaceae*)
MWT 4°C (40°F). A slightly tender evergreen shrub from the Mediterranean generally known as myrtle. With fragrant polished leaves and white flowers in summer they can be useful in cool conditions where they are not hardy in the open. Preferably pot and re-pot in spring in lime-free soil-based compost. Prune in February when necessary. They are best outside in semi-shade in summer. *M. communis*, ultimately up to 4.5m (15ft), and its smaller variegated form; *M. c. tarentina* is a dwarf and compact variety which can be grown in small pots.

NANDINA (*Berberidaceae*)
MWT 4°C (40°F). A decorative evergreen bamboo-like plant from China and Japan with attractive reddish young leaves. It can be planted out in a cold conservatory. *N. domestica*, 90cm–1.8m (3–6ft).

NARCISSUS (*Amaryllidaceae*)
Cold. All the daffodils and narcissi can be grown in pots for early colour and

scent where there is little or no heat. The ones that are naturally early are perhaps the most rewarding. They can be potted in virtually any compost in August and September and brought into the conservatory from Christmas onwards. One can put a double layer of bulbs in a reasonably sized pot to make a splash of colour. What to choose is a matter of personal choice. I often try out new kinds in this way and then plant them in the garden.

NEOREGELIA (*Bromeliaceae*)
MWT 10°C (50°F). Evergreen epiphytic urn plants with brilliantly coloured centres at flowering time. They are grown as house plants and the best known is *N. carolinae* 'Tricolor' with cream and green striped leaves and a scarlet centre for some months when mature. They can be grown in equal quantities of leaf mould, peat and sand or a soil-less compost with added perlite. Always keep the central cup filled with water and the roots moist. They like bright light with some sun. The rosette that has flowered will die but a young one should develop at the base of the plant. *N. concentrica* has a purple centre and others are red or pink. See BROMELIADS.

NEPHROLEPIS (*Oleandraceae*)
MWT 10°C (50°F). A very useful and domesticated fern that is particularly effective in hanging baskets. *N. exaltata*, the Boston fern, has many varieties with fringed fronds. *N. cordifolia* is more upright. For culture see FERNS.

NERINE (*Amaryllidaceae*)
MWT 4°C (40°F). Very handsome South African bulbs with umbels of irridescent flowers in autumn. Pot in August in J.I.P.1 singly or three to a 13cm (5in) pot, leaving the top of the bulbs exposed. Water after potting but not again until growth shows. They flower best when established so only re-pot after three years. Water sparingly until growing strongly and then freely until the leaves start to yellow in May. Dry off gradually and keep in sun during the summer with only an occasional watering to prevent complete dessication. They grow in poor sandy soils in nature and do not need feeding. Only freedom from frost is necessary for any of the hybrid nerines. Increase by offsets which are freely produced. They are very beautiful cut flowers especially under artifical light. Dozens of magnificent hybrids are available from a specialist grower. Hardy nerines that can be grown outside may also be grown in unheated conservatories. They are dormant in winter and should be planted between November and February. *N. bowdenii* is the hardy outdoor nerine with pink flowers. *N. b.* 'Fenwick's variety' is a deeper pink and taller, both flower in October, around 60cm (2ft). There are also other smaller species. Greenhouse nerines also flower in autumn, mainly in October but are dormant during June, July and August. The flowers develop before the leaves. *N. sarniensis* (the Guernsey lily) is a true species, orange scarlet, 38cm (15in). *N.* 'Fothergillii Major', flowering in August and *N.corusca major* are closely

related to it, and many hundreds of named hybrids have been bred from this and other species. They come in every possible shade of red, pink and white and have from eight to seventeen florets on a single stalk, 38–63cm (15–25in) tall. Most flower in October. The choice must be a personal one.

NERIUM (*Apocynaceae*)
MWT 40°C (40°F). Oleanders are attractive evergreen flowering shrubs from the Mediterranean. Every part of the plant is very poisonous. They start flowering when small but ultimately become too large. Grow in J.I.P.2 or 3 or other rich compost. Water freely from May to September and little from November to March. To ensure flowering remove small sideshoots if they appear just below the flower buds before these have expanded. Feed during summer. Flowers develop on previous year's shoots so prune lightly immediately after flowering. They can be raised from seed but the best kinds are increased by cuttings of well-ripened shoots which can be rooted in water in summer. Hybrids of *N. oleander* with single or double flowers, crimson, rose, apricot and white, summer, 1.8–3.6m (6–12ft).

NIEREMBERGIA (*Solanaceae*)
MWT 4°C (40°F). A small perennial from the Argentine which makes a good pot plant when grown as a biennial. Sown in summer or autumn they will flower for quite a long time the following summer. They have tiny leaves and a mass of flowers much like a campanula. *N. caerulea* (syn. *N. hippomanica*), violet-blue, summer, 20–38cm (8–15in).

NOLINA see BEAUCARNEA

NORFOLK ISLAND PINE see ARAUCARIA

NOTOCACTUS (*Cactaceae*)
MWT 10°C (50°F). South American cacti worth growing for their attractive spine formations. They mostly have yellow flowers when mature. *N. leninghausii*, charming golden spines on a columnar cactus; *N. magnificus* and *N. scopa* are both good. For culture see CACTI.

NYMPHAEA (*Nymphaeaceae*)
MWT 16°C (60°F). Tropical water-lilies can be grown in tubs or bowls to provide an exotic touch in a warm conservatory. They are gross feeders and need about a bushel of soil each to give of their best. I have not grown them myself but am assured that they can be rewarding. Plant in spring. If they are dry tubers pot them singly in small pots of loam soil and stand these in 5in (13cm) of water which should be 19°C (65°F). When the floating leaves appear they can be planted properly. For this just cover the bottom of the receptacle with coarse bone meal and on top of this put 10–13cm (4–5in) of plain loam soil. If well-decayed cow manure is available use this instead of the bone meal. In either case make sure that it is entirely covered with loam and does not

contaminate the water. Ideally water-lilies are planted in a container 30cm (1ft) deep and 60cm (2ft) square that is lowered into a deeper pool. In any case add water gradually over some days. Sudden drenching in cold tap water is not appreciated. The depth of the water should be about 30cm (1ft). They need a sunny position.

ODONTOGLOSSUM (*Orchidaceae*)
MWT 10°C (50°F).The easiest members of this family of orchids are worth considering in a conservatory. They come from the high mountain ranges of northern South America and need more humidity and ventilation than most plants. O. *bictoniense* from Guatemala is a tall plant flowering in late summer while O. *cervantesii* from Mexico is quite dwarf and must never be dry. See ORCHIDS.

OLIVERANTHUS see ECHEVERIA

OPLISMENUS (*Gramineae*)
MWT 10°C (50°F). Elegant variegated grass that trails like tradescantia. It is good in hanging baskets or in small pots at the edge of staging. Grow in soil-based compost in full light. Renew yearly from cuttings in spring or summer putting half a dozen in a small pot in a plastic bag. Treat them as one plant when rooted. O. *hirtellus* 'Variegatus', small white striped leaves which take on pink and purple colouring in strong light.

ORCHIDS
Until fairly recently gardening books gave the impression that no ordinary person could re-pot an orchid. It was implied that they could only be grown in specially built greenhouses in high temperatures and with a professional gardener damping down the floor several times a day. Now we are urged to grow them on our window sills. Modern methods of propagation and culture have brought this vast and fascinating family of plants within the sights of many more people. Nevertheless they remain different in lifestyle from other plants. If there is no greenhouse back-up to the conservatory I should forget about orchids unless you are one of those who have succeeded in growing them indoors. Orchids have to be understood. They are mostly epiphytic in nature even if we grow them in pots and they will withold their wonderful flowers unless one recognises and allows for their unique timing and growing mechanisms. It is not that they are difficult but we have to adapt to their preferences rather than the other way round. Having said that, anyone can grow PLEIONES MWT 4°C (40°F) and CYMBIDIUMS 7°C (45°F). Otherwise 10°C (50°F) is really the minimum winter temperature and 13°C (55°F) easier for most orchids. Effective shading and humidity are also necessary. They do, however, combine well with bromeliads and a conservatory of these two plant families alone would be a very interesting and rewarding place.

The specialist nurserymen who sell orchids are accustomed to giving a certain amount of instruction to their clients and also sell suitable compost mixtures. It is certainly wise to start with flowering-sized plants already established in their pots. Indeed,you may wish to choose them when actually in flower. They will not then need re-potting for a year, by which time they will be better understood, or dead. Modern potting methods are not difficult. The orchids in this book are COELOGYNE, CYMBIDIUM, DENDROBIUM, EPIDENDRUM, ODONTOGLOSSUM, PAPHIOPEDILUM and PLEIONE.

PACHYPHYTUM (*Crassulaceae*)
MWT 7°C (45°F). Succulent plants from Mexico with rounded leaves like sugar almonds. They are closely related to ECHEVERIA and need the same treatment. *P. oviferum*, globular leaves with white bloom and reddish flowers in summer is the most often seen.

PACHYSTACHYS (*Acanthaceae*)
MWT 16°C (60°F). A small bushy plant from Brazil related to *Jacobinia*, with showy terminal flower spikes consisting of yellow bracts from which emerge small white flowers. It is a tropical house plant which flowers much of the year in reasonable warmth and shaded from summer sun. It can be grown in soil or peat composts. Cuttings of non-flowering shoots will root in summer. *P. lutea*, sometimes known as the 'lollipop plant'.

PALMS (*Palmae*)
The palm family is an enormous one and they are mainly tropical plants. The form of their leaves is either a frond like a fern which is called pinnate or like a fan with fingers which is called palmate. Although often ultimately of tree size palms only have a single growing point at the top of the stem and if this is damaged they will die. Our winters are not always kind and we tend to think of them as rather battered and unnatural objects in our landscape. Indoors, however, they are enjoying a revival. They are mostly slow-growing in the early stages and large specimens are expensive. There is, however, a good choice of young plants. It can be a good idea for these to spend a year or two in the home before going into a cool conservatory. The move should be made in the summer.

Amongst the fern-leaved palms the most familiar are the howeas (often called kentias). *H. forsteriana* is the Victorian parlour palm and a mainstay of palm courts and municipal decoration to this day. *H. belmoreana* is slightly more spreading but similar. These must have shade in summer and are noted for their tolerance of the discomforts of social life. They would prefer a minimum of 10°C (50°F) in winter but are good at putting up with varying conditions. Then there is the other 'parlour palm' *Chamaedorea elegans* (syn. *Collinia elegans*) which is a popular house plant today. This is a small palm that needs higher temperatures and is better for those half living-room and half conservatory situations. It will stand lower temperatures if accustomed to them gradually but is noted for its survival of shade and central heating. In America *Chamaedorea erumpens* is more favoured. This is known as the bamboo palm and has several thin stems and small fronds. *C. Savrittzii* is another palm of this kind. They are said to survive a minimum winter temperature of 4°C (40°F) and are available Britain but I have no experience of growing them. A hardier type of palm with pinnate fronds is *Rhopalostylis bauerii*, known as the feather duster palm from Norfolk Island. There is also *R. sapida*, the 'Nikau' palm from New Zealand. The date palms are called *Phoenix* and have pinnate leaves of a rather bristly nature. The most familiar in pots is the pygmy date palm *P. roebelini* but this is not recommended for conservatories as it prefers higher temperatures in winter and considerable humidity. *P. canariensis* from the Canary Islands is the most favoured and should be all right so long as frost is excluded. It eventually grows big and heavy even in a tub. *P. rupicola* (the cliff date) is as graceful as any and *P. reclinata* from Senegal can also be grown. It forms suckers and is of the clustering clump-forming kind.

In warm coastal places in Britain and occasionally inland one sees the hardiest fan-leaved palm, *Trachycarpus Fortunei* (syn. *Chamaerops excelsa*). *Chamaerops humilis* a smaller relative from southern Europe, is more suitable for the conservatory. This can be kept to a single stem or allowed to cluster. Another palm-like plant one often sees in Cornwall is *Cordyline australis* (which see). This is not a palm. *Livistona* is a genus of fan-leaved palms for low temperatures. *L. chinensis* is the most often available but *L. australis* is also good. Washingtonias are another possibility but need to be kept almost dry in winter when temperatures are low. A miniature palm much prized in Japan is the variegated form of *Rhapisexcelsa*. This has clustered stems of small palmate white striped fronds.

Palms resent root disturbance and should be carefully re-potted in spring when the pots are full of roots. Soil-based compost with some added peat and very good drainage is needed. Avoid subjecting them to sudden and violent fluctuations of both light and heat. In nature palms usually grow on the margins of forest and under a high canopy of trees where there is moist air and shade. They need ample water in summer and to be kept moist always. A baking from the sun in stuffy conditions is not their scene. All can stand outside in a sheltered place in summer if kept well watered.

PAMIANTHE (*Amaryllidaceae*)
MWT 13°C (55°F). An exotic bulbous plant from the Peruvian Andes for those who seek the rare (*Plate 55*). It is closely related to the daffodil-like *Hymenocallis* but more distinguished. Grow in J.I.P.2 with a little added peat and do not re-pot until unavoidable but feed when growing strongly. It can be raised from seed but could take many years to flower. It also increases by

stolons. The large scented flowers appear in spring. *P. peruviana*, white flowers striped with pale green on stalks up to 60cm (2ft).

PANICUM see OPLISMENUS

PANSY see VIOLA

PAPHIOPEDILUM (*Orchidaceae*)
MWT 13°C (55°F). Terrestrial orchids from tropical Asia. They do not have pseudobulbs and need to be kept evenly moist and shaded from sunshine throughout the year. They have an oriental charm and the waxy flowers are long-lasting. They usually have single flowers on a stem which will need a wire support for the larger hybrids. They are not for the casual, indeed they can look at one with some disdain! *P. callosum*, mottled leaves, white and green flower suffused reddish purple; *P. insigne*, green leaves, white and green spotted and suffused with brown. *P. venustum*, marbled leaves, white and green with pink suffusion and brown spots. There are many modern hybrids of improved vigour, colour and substance of which *P. Honey Gorse* 'Sunshine' is an example, with a yellow and green flower. Those flowering in winter are perhaps the most valuable. See also ORCHIDS.

PASSIFLORA (*Passifloraceae*)
Cold to warm. The passion flower is a vigorous tendril climber from South America. *P. caerulea* and its cultivar 'Constance Elliott' are white with handsome blue and purple filaments and can be grown without heat. *P. x allardii*, white shaded pink with blue filaments, needs some heat. *P. racemosa* has red flowers. They can be used to create shade in summer and pruned back to within two buds of old wood in winter. They may be grown in tubs for a time and must have good drainage. Use J.I.P.1 or 2. Cuttings with a heel taken in spring root readily. *P. caerulea* flowers when young and can be grown in a pot. The flowers appear through the summer and are of fascinating construction. Water freely while growing strongly but very little in winter. Re-pot yearly in spring and high potash feed in summer. *P. quadrangularis (Plate 56)*, the giant grenadilla, has the most impressive flowers and also fruit but needs a really warm conservatory throughout the year.

PEDILANTHUS (*Euphorbiaceae*)
MWT 13°C (55°F). Curious succulent shrubs from South America with strange zigzag growth like ricrac embroidery. They are good for warm conditions with dry air and sunlight. Beware of over-watering and avoid getting the sap near the eyes or on the skin. Treat like succulents using a soil-based compost with extra sand or grit. Do not re-pot until essential. Tip cuttings will root in summer. Dip them in water to stop the stems bleeding and dry before inserting. *P. tithymaloides* 'Smallii' is the one usually grown, particularly its variegated form with paler margins to the leaves.

PELARGONIUM (*Geraniaceae*)
Frost-free but MWT 7°C (45°F) better. This group of plants commonly, but wrongly, known as geraniums, are the true friends of all conservatory owners. We welcome adaptable plants prepared to flower both early and late, and indeed all the time, if there is a modicum of warmth and light. Those who find the pelargoniums boring have not penetrated very deeply into this most varied group of plants.

The zonal pelargoniums, famous for bedding out and closely matching the colour of a guardsman's tunic or tinned salmon, are loyal supporters even in poor summers. There are many others too that can be excellent in window boxes and patio pots but hundreds of cultivars only give of their best with the protection of glass and they have a colour range covering all but the blues and deep yellows. They come in many shapes and sizes, with single and double flowers as well as the more exotic rosebud or starry shapes. Zonal pelargoniums can be induced to flower at any time of year, but their colours will not be true with poor winter light. Most zonals can grow quite large and are sometimes trained as standards, which takes a couple of years. They can even be used to cover conservatory walls. There are also smaller kinds known as dwarfs and miniatures. These are much more convenient on the windowsill or anywhere where space is limited. Many have dark green or even blackish leaves. A few have little grace but most are delightful.

Ivy-leaved pelargoniums are familiar to all and much used in hanging baskets and window boxes. They are at their best in a slightly warmer and drier climate than ours but make a particularly brave show in towns and places sheltered from the wind. Their disadvantage under glass is that they do not share the zonal's remarkable freedom from greenfly. Here too there are smaller kinds which add variety and interest. The ivy-leaved kinds do not flower all the year though they keep going throughout the summer. They are sometimes used to clothe a wall under glass.

There is no more Victorian plant than the regal pelargonium with its smooth rounded leaves and a bountiful mass of frilly bloom for much of the summer. When very well-grown and kept from year to year they become large and impressive plants, excellent for tubs in a large conservatory, but in most circumstances young plants are better. Their only vice is that they are attractive to white fly. Fortunately they are easily renewed yearly from cuttings and can be kept small. There are some good miniature regals and also miniature angel pelargoniums. These have smaller pansy-shaped flowers and great charm.

The commonest 'geranium' bought in the nearest market can actually cost more than the very best from specialist nurseries. These have catalogues and send out small plants or cuttings by mail order. If bought in the spring they quickly grow into flowering plants. The main difficulty is knowing what to order amongst the hundreds offered. Visits to nurseries and flower shows are very helpful.

The great thing about this group is that almost any shoot will root as a cutting at almost any time of year. Late summer is a good time so that they are well rooted and potted separately before the bad weather. The constant reproduction from cuttings has led to much virus infection in zonal pelargoniums, and good virus-free seed-raised strains are now available. These need early sowing in warmth and are slow to flower but can be increased from cuttings after the first season. Otherwise begin by buying new plants in April or May and re-pot in 13cm (5in) pots using J.I.P.2 or whatever compost you are using generally. The regal types need more feeding than the others, with a potash-based fertiliser such as Phostrogen. I list a few suggestions in the various categories. *Zonals*: 'Beatrix Little', vermillion; 'Caledonia', mauve pink; 'Mr. Wren', red with white margin; 'Highfields Festival', pale rose pink; 'Regina', pink shading to salmon; 'Caroline Schmidt', silver variegated leaf, red flower; *Miniatures and Dwarfs*: 'Bath Beauty', dark leaf, salmon; 'Improved Kleine Liebling', cherry pink; 'Granny Hewitt', scarlet; 'Snow Flake', white. *Ivy-leaved Pelargoniums*: 'Berliner Balkon', pink; 'L'Elegante', leaves edged white, flowers white with purple veins; 'Lilac Gem', mauve with scented foliage; 'Rouletta', white with crimson edges and stripes. *Miniature Ivy-leaved Pelargoniums*: 'Red Cascade', cherry red; 'Sugar Baby' (syn. 'Pink Gay Baby'), prostrate with double pink flowers. *Regal Pelargoniums*: 'Aztec', white feathered red and brown; 'Destiny', pure white; 'Grand Slam', rose red with violet marking; 'Lavender Grand Slam,' lavender violet; 'Princess of Wales', strawberry with white frilly edges. *Scented-leaved Species*: *P. crispum* 'Variegatum', lemon-scented; *P. graveolens* 'Lady Plymouth', rose-lemon scent and very pretty variegated leaves.

PELLAEA (*Sinopteridaceae*)
MWT 7°C (45°F). The button fern has small circular glossy dark green leaflets and can be used as ground cover in shady parts of a cool conservatory. *P. rotundifolia*, 15cm (6in). For culture see FERNS.

PENTAPTERYGIUM see AGAPETES

PENTAS (*Rubiaceae*)
MWT 13°C (55°F). Soft-wooded shrubs from Africa with terminal clusters of starry flowers. In warm climates they flower for much of the year. They are inclined to flop and should be kept moist at all times and pinched to make a bushy plant. Seed is available of compact hybrids in various colours. Grow in J.I.P.2 and feed when the pots are full of roots. Re-pot and cut back in spring. Increase from tip cuttings. *P. lanceolata*, pale purple, up to 60cm (2ft). Also dwarf hybrids, crimson, pink and white, 45cm (18in).

PEPEROMIA (*Piperaceae*)
MWT 13°C (55°F). Popular small evergreen foliage plants from South America with attractive fleshy leaves. They provide a variety of low-growing plants for

warm shady positions in reasonably moist air. They do not need much root room and do best in peat-based composts. Increase by tip cuttings in warmth. *P. argyreia*, the water-melon peperomia, has heart-shaped leaves with bands of silver; *P. obtusifolia* has glossy rounded leaves and purple stems and comes in several variegated forms; *P. magnoliifolia* 'Variegata' is a bushy plant with glossy oval leaves and creamy markings; *P. scandens* 'Variegata' is a climbing form with heart-shaped leaves with paler margins. There are many others. The flowers are unimportant.

PETREA (*Verbenaceae*)
MWT 13°C (55°F). Beautiful twining climber from South America with metallic violet flowers (*Plate 57*). Available as seed. It is suitable for hot dry conditions and needs good drainage. It can be grown in soil-based compost in pots or planted out and flowers from March to June. Cuttings will root in warmth. *P. volubilis* (purple wreath) ultimately tall.

PETUNIA (*Solanaceae*)
Cold. Tender perennials grown as half-hardy annuals to flower from June to October. They are very good for patio pots, window boxes and as a quick filler in sunny positions. One can still get single colours and double and fringed flowers to satisfy a particular whim. Sow in March or early April, preferably with extra warmth. They need sunshine and constant moisture at the roots to do well. Use John Innes composts or similar. Single and double F.1 hybrids with flowers of every colour and size. The single large-flowered fringed types and the large and small double hybrids benefit most from glass protection.

PHARBITIS see IPOMOEA

PHILODENDRON (*Araceae*)
16°C (60°F). Handsome evergreen foliage plants from the tropical rain forests of Central and South America. In nature they mostly climb and have aerial roots in addition to roots in the ground. They can be grown in either soil-based or peat-based composts and will need shade from April to October. A single large plant in a large container is perhaps the most impressive way of growing them. *P. bipinnatifidum* and the rather similar *P. selloum*, with large divided glossy leaves up to 38cm (15in) long, are my favourites, but there are many to choose from. *P.* 'Burgundy' with purplish red arrow-shaped leaves provides a contrast. There are also smaller climbing types like *P. scandens* with small heart-shaped leaves, which can climb up a mossy pole.

PHOENIX (*Palmae*)
MWT 10°C (50°F). Palms with pinnate leaves which include the date palm *P. dactylifera*. For culture see under PALMS. *P. canariensis* is the hardiest and worth growing where frost is excluded. It is a rather bristly plant to be found in garden centres. It eventually grows big and heavy even in a tub. *P. roebelinii* is

o. *Datura suaveolens* and *D.* 'Grand Marnier'. 41. *Dendrobium* hybrid.

2. *Echeveria gibbiflora*. 43. *Echeveria peacockii nummulosa*.

4. *Echeveria pulidonis lutea*. 45. *Epiphyllum* hybrid.

46. *Epiphyllum* hybrid.

47. *Eranthemum pulchellum.*

48. *Hoya imperialis.*

49. *Ipomoea rubrocaerulea.*

50. *Kalanchoe pumila.*

51. *Lagerstroemia indica.*

. Lapageria rosea 'Alba'.

53. Medinilla magnifica.

Mimulus glutinosus.

55. Pamianthe peruviana.

Passiflora quadrangularis.

57. Petrea volubilis.

58. *Pleione* hybrid.

59. *Plumbago capensis.*

60. *Salvia involucrata* 'Bethellii'.

61. *Schizanthus pinnatus* hybrid.

62. *Stephanotis floribunda.*

63. *Streptosolen jamesonii.*

the handsome miniature palm most familiar in pots but really needs a higher temperature in winter and a moist atmosphere. *P. rupicola* (the cliff date) is as graceful as any and *P. reclinata* from Senegal can also be grown. It forms suckers and is of the clustering clump-forming type.

PHYLLITIS (*Aspleniaceae*)
Cold. The hart's tongue fern is an easily grown hardy evergreen fern with plain leathery fronds of a pale bright green with black stalks. There are varieties with frilled edges to the fronds which can decorate an unheated and shady conservatory. For culture see FERNS. The rhizomes can be divided in spring. *P. scolopendrium* varieties.

PILEA (*Urticaceae*)
MWT 13°C (55°F). Small foliage house plants from tropical America with variously textured and prettily marked leaves. They are at their best when young and useful grouped together as ground-cover in a large container in half-shade. Increase from cuttings in summer. Grow in peat-based compost and keep very moist in summer and less so in winter. *P. cadierei* (aluminium plant) up to 30cm (1ft); *P. involucrata* 'Moon Valley' about 15cm (6in); *P. microphylla* (syn. *P. muscosa*) is called artillery plant because it shoots its pollen about. This is a miniature fern-like plant with tiny leaves.

PITTOSPORUM (*Pittosporaceae*)
Frost-free. Slightly tender evergreen trees and shrubs from China, Japan and New Zealand that are hardy in some parts of the country. Although ultimately large all are decorative when young and can be useful in the cold or poorly heated conservatory. *P. tobira*, with whirls of polished green leaves and scented cream flowers in summer, grows quickly from seed. Grow in soil-based compost. *P. eugenioides*, pale green crinkled leaves, and *P. e.* 'Variegatum', with white markings; *P. tenuifolium* and its various coloured leaf forms with silver and mauve markings; *P. tobira* is slightly more tender and also has a variegated form with white markings.

PLATYCERIUM (*Polypodiaceae*)
MWT 7°C (45°F). Epiphytic ferns mainly from rain forests in tropical Australia and Asia. They are very striking and not difficult. When young they can be in pots but in nature they attach themselves to the bark of tall trees. Their flattened sterile fronds catch falling detritus while the decorative horned fertile fronds spread out below. The roots can be wrapped in peat and sphagnum moss and tied to a piece of bark or wood and fixed to the wall. They can also be grown in wooden orchid baskets. *P. bifurcatum* is the species usually offered and the easiest to grow.

PLECTRANTHUS (*Labiatae*)
MWT 13°C (55°F). Small creeping foliage plants related to coleus that are used

to trail in hanging baskets. They need good light and constant moisture. Grow in soil-based compost. Increase by tip cuttings at any time. *P. coleiodes* 'Marginatus' has heart-shaped leaves with white margins; *P. oertendahlii* is similar with smaller slightly felted bronze green leaves with purple undersides.

PLEIONE (*Orchidaceae*)
Cold. Small terrestrial orchids with beautiful flowers on 8cm (3in) stalks in March and April. They can stand outdoors in a shady place from the end of May to November and are kept quite dry in winter. For those prepared to water them in summer this is an easy plant from high in the Himalayas where they grow in moss at the feet and on the trunks of trees. I have grown them in J.I.P.2, orchid compost, and a mixture of ground bark and soil. They seem totally indifferent but do need re-potting every other year. Start with three in an 8cm (3in) pot. *P. formosana*, varying shades of rosy-lilac with fringed cream lip spotted with brown. There are many hybrids and other kinds which may be more tender (*Plate 58*).

PLEOMELE (*Liliaceae*)
MWT 16°C (60°F). A decorative variegated shrub much seen in tropical countries but inclined to drop its leaves. *P. reflexa* 'Variegata' is known as 'song of India' and should really be called *Dracaena reflexa* 'Variegata'. For culture see DRACAENA.

PLUMBAGO (*Plumbaginaceae*)
MWT 7°C (45°F). A favourite conservatory climbing shrub from South Africa with phlox-like flowers for many weeks in summer. Grown from seed it will flower in eighteen months in a pot. Grow in J.I.P.2 or 3. It can also be increased by cuttings in summer. It is best planted out against a wall. *P. capensis*, pale blue (*Plate 59*) and *P. c.* 'Alba' white; *P. rosea* from tropical Asia with rose-red flowers in winter needs MWT 13°C (55°F).

PODOCARPUS (*Podocarpaceae*)
MWT 10°C (50°F). A Chinese conifer with narrow leathery leaves known as Buddhist pine. It makes a good pot plant. Use soil- based compost and do not over-pot. Water moderately and feed when growing actively. Shade from hot sun. *P. macrophyllus*, slow-growing to 1.5–1.8m (5–6ft).

POINSETTIA see EUPHORBIA

POLYGALA (*Polygalaceae*)
MWT 4°C (40°F). Easily grown small evergreen South African shrub with magenta pea flowers in late spring. Grow in J.I.P.2 or similar compost. Prune hard back after flowering. Water freely in summer and keep just moist in winter. It can be plunged outdoors after flowering until October. Re-pot in early spring. Increase by cuttings of young shoots in spring. *P. myrtifolia grandiflora*, ultimately 1.2–1.8m (4–6ft).

POLYPODIUM (*Polypodiaceae*)
MWT 10°C (50°F). Handsome ferns from tropical America and Australia related to our native *P. vulgare*. Like it they appreciate good drainage and some lime in the soil. For culture see FERNS. *P. aureum* (syn. *Phlebodium aureum*) with bluish fronds and *P. a.* 'Mandaianum' with blue wavy-edged fronds, both up to 60cm (2ft).

POLYSTICHUM (*Aspidiaceae*)
MWT 13°C (55°F). One small variety of this fern is grown as a house plant and is active all the year in warmth and shade. For culture see FERNS. *P. tsus-simense* has delicate fronds some 15cm (6in) long.

PORTULACARIA (*Portulaceae*)
MWT 10°C (50°F). Succulent shrub from South Africa known as elephant bush. It has a curiously artificial look with black stems and glossy bead-like leaves. It is happy in sunny positions and dry air. Grow in soil-based compost with added grit and keep watered as it drops its leaves in drought. *P. afra*, ultimately a tall bush, its variegated form is odd but ugly.

POTHOS see SCINDAPSUS

PRAYER PLANT see MARANTA

PRIMULA (*Primulaceae*)
Cold to cool. A delightful group of plants to raise from seed for flowering in winter and spring in cool conditions. Even without heat alpine primulas and the highly coloured cultivars of the primrose may be grown in pots for winter decoration. *P. acaulis* (primrose) sown in May and June in a cold frame can be grown in shade outdoors until autumn. Keep them watered and protected from slugs and pot up in October, returning them to the garden in spring. *P. auricula* comes in various forms and quite good ones can be raised from seed. Selected forms with white powdered leaves and flowers are known as 'Show' auriculas and would be spoiled by rain. They are available from specialists and grown in cool protected conditions. They are expensive but fascinating. There are several alpine primulas with a similar type of smooth powdered leaf and clusters of mauve flowers in spring that can be grown in pans of gritty soil and brought into the conservatory to bloom. *P. x kewensis* is a yellow primula flowering in spring that is easily raised from seed sown a year previously. The better known *P. malacoides* in various shades of mauve, white and cherry red can be sown from April to June to flower in late winter. The more tender *P. obconica* is sown in April and May and flowers continuously once it starts but some people are allergic to it.

PROSTANTHERA (*Labiatae*)
MWT 4°C (40°F). Evergreen shrubs from Australia with aromatic foliage and purple, lilac or white flowers in late winter and spring. They flower when

young and can be grown in pots. They prefer peaty lime-free compost. They are easily increased by cuttings or raised from seed. They are hardy in Cornwall. *P. melissifolia parviflora*, *P. sieberi* and *P. rotundifolia* all have lilac or purple flowers in spring and *P. nivea* is white. Although ultimately up to 2.4m (8ft) tall they flower at 45cm (18in).

PTERIS (*Pteridaceae*)
MWT 10°C (50°F). Slightly tender ferns with finely divided fronds that have long been popular as temporary house plants. In warmth they grow all the year round. They must never be dry at the roots or exposed to direct sunlight. Although normally seen in very small pots they are more impressive if allowed more space. For culture see FERNS. *P. cretica* and its variety *P. c.* 'Albo-lineata' with a whitish variegation; *P. tremula* from New Zealand is larger with fronds up to 60cm (2ft) long.

PUNICA (*Punicaceae*)
MWT 4°C (40°F). The pomegranate is a deciduous shrub with small glossy leaves and scarlet flowers in late summer. There is a miniature kind which flowers the first year from seed. Grow in J.I.P.2 or similar compost. Water freely in summer and keep in full sun. Keep just moist in winter. Prune lightly after flowering. Increase by cuttings of half-ripe shoots in July or raise from seed in spring. *P. granatum* and its variety 'Nana' which starts flowering at 8cm (3in) high.

PYRETHRUM (*Compositae*)
MWT 4°C (40°F). A half-hardy shrubby perennial from the Canary Islands known as 'Silver Lace' is easily raised from seed. The finely cut silver foliage is a useful foil for bright colours in the conservatory. It can also be increased by cuttings. Grow in soil-based composts. Remove the flowering stems before they develop. *P. ptarmacifolium* (syn. *Tanacetum ptarmacifolium*) grows 30cm (1ft) in the first season.

RAT'S TAIL CACTUS see APOROCACTUS

REBUTIA (*Cactaceae*)
MWT 4°C (40°F). Easily grown and free-flowering small clustering cacti from high altitudes in Argentina and Bolivia with red or yellow flowers in early spring. Shade from hot sun in summer. For culture see CACTI. Rebutias can flower in one year from seed and are readily increased by rooting offsets. They hybridize freely and the names are only important to the specialist.

RECHSTEINERIA (*Gesneriaceae*)
MWT 10°C (50°F). Fascinating tuberous plant, originally from Brazil. *R. leucotricha* has delightful furry silver leaves and apricot tubular flowers in summer. It can be grown like a tuberous begonia but in brighter light and a

drier atmosphere. Pot and re-pot yearly in March in J.I.P.2 or any well-drained mixture. Dry off in autumn and keep quite dry from November to March. Seed is also available. *R. cardinalis* with orange-scarlet flowers and green velvety leaves is often sold as a pot plant. This was formerly known as *Gesneria cardinalis* and can be grown in the same way.

REHMANNIA (*Scrophulariaceae*)
MWT 4°C (40°F). Unusual herbaceous plant from China like a refined foxglove. Raise from seed in spring. It is useful in ground beds under glass where it seeds itself. *R. angulata*, various rosy shades, 30–60cm (1–2ft).

RHAPIS (*Palmae*)
MWT 4°C (40°F). Slow-growing fan palms from Japan. *R. excelsa* and variegated form. For culture see PALMS.

RHIPSALIDOPSIS (*Cactaceae*)
MWT 13°C (55°F). These epiphytic jungle cacti like good light but not sun and plenty of water when growing. Keep drier for a week or two after flowering or if the temperature is too low in winter. They prefer room temperature all the year round. If grown in peat-based compost feed occasionally all the year. If grown in soil-based compost only feed in very early spring until flowers open. Use a tomato fertiliser. *R. gaertneri*, the Easter cactus (formerly *Schlumbergera gaertneri*), is the best known. It has orange-scarlet flowers in spring. *R. rosea* with rose-pink starlike flowers late spring is the gem of the family and there are hybrids between these two plants.

RHIPSALIS (*Cactaceae*)
MWT 10°C (50°F). Epiphytic jungle cacti known as mistletoe cacti because they look like mistletoe if one ignores every botanical fact. These are basket plants for those intrigued by the curious. *R. cassutha*, *R. cereuscula* and *R. pilocarpa* all have a tangle of pendulous narrow green stems. In time they will have small, sweet-smelling, starry flowers followed by berries. Grow in orchid compost or peat-based compost with one third added sharp sand or perlite. *R. cassutha*, green flowers, white berries; *R. cereuscula*, white flowers, white berries; *R. pilocarpa*, white flowers, red berries. All hang up to 60cm (2ft).

RHODOCHITON (*Scrophulariaceae*)
MWT 7°C (45°F). Charming Mexican climber related to MAURANDIA and needing the same treatment. It flowers the first season from seed and is usually grown as an annual. The delightful pendulous flowers are best seen from below. *R. volubile*, dark red flowers with rosy bracts, June, to 3m (10ft).

RHODODENDRON (*Ericaceae*)
MWT 7°C (45°F). The small evergreen flowering shrubs we think of as 'Indian azaleas' are hybrids of *R. simsii*, mostly raised in Belgium and sold in bud from November to March. They will probably have been grown in a mixture of peat

and leafmould and should be soaked in a bucket if they are dry. After that keep steadily moist but not sodden. After flowering remove dead blooms, trim straggling shoots and re-pot when necessary in April. Plunge outdoors in light shade from June to October but never allow to dry. The other popular indoor azalea is R. *obtusum* and its varieties from Japan. These have smaller pink flowers and shiny leaves and are hardier and can be planted out in the garden if your soil is lime-free. They all need lime-free soil and should be watered with rain water in hard water districts. It is also possible to grow some of the tender scented Himalayan rhododendrons in a cool conservatory but they are not easy to keep healthy. R. *fragrantissimum*, white tinged pink; 'Countess of Haddington', similar and 'Lady Alice Fitzwilliam', white, ultimately large. For a higher temperature new species have been introduced from New Guinea but a specialist nursery should be consulted.

RHOEO (*Commelinaceae*)
MWT 16°C (60°F). Evergreen plant from tropical America related to tradescantia. It is a fairly tolerant house plant and forms a rosette of stiff leaves up to 30cm (1ft) long with reddish purple undersides. Old plants develop a stem and offsets appear at the base which can be removed when they have made some roots. It has inconspicuous flowers in its centre contained in purplish bracts. These give rise to local names such as 'Moses in the cradle' and 'three men in a boat'. It can be grown in soil or peat-based compost. R. *spathacea* (syn. R. *discolor*) and R. *s.* 'Variegata' with bright yellow striped leaves.

RHOICISSUS (*Vitidaceae*)
MWT 10°C (50°F). Evergreen tendril climber from tropical Africa which is an adaptable house plant and can be useful in shady and fairly warm conditions to make a screen. It can be severely pruned if necessary. Grow in J.I.P.2 and re-pot yearly in spring until the right size is reached. Then top-dress in spring and feed in summer. R. *capensis*, 1.2–1.8m (4–6ft).

ROCHEA (*Crassulaceae*)
MWT 7°C (45°F). Succulent sub-shrub from South Africa with clustered heads of scarlet flowers in early summer. This used to be a popular commercial flowering pot plant but is slower to reach the flowering stage than its rivals today. Cuttings root readily in spring but only flower in the following summer. Pinch out tips to make bushy plants. Grow in J.I.P.2 with a little sharp sand added and flower in 13 or 15cm (5 or 6in) pots. Feed after first season. After flowering cut old flowering stems hard back in the hope that sideshoots will flower the following year. The flower stems may need some support. R. *coccinea* (syn. *Crassula coccinea*), scarlet, early summer, 30cm (1ft). R. *falcata* see *Crassula falcata*.

ROSA (*Rosaceae*)
Cold or cool. Although hardy, it is possible to grow roses under glass and miniature roses have become fashionable temporary pot plants. 'The Fairy

Rose' actually flowers in ten weeks from seed. Floribundas and dwarf polyanthas can be grown in pots for early flowers. The greenfly, the mildew, the thorns and the constant busy round of the rose grower are not for me. However, potted very firmly in J.I.P.3 in autumn roses can be plunged outside until after Christmas unless the weather is severe. Then prune hard back to outside buds and bring inside. Water very little until growth starts. When growing they will appreciate spraying with clear water each morning in warm weather. Without heat they should flower in April and May. By June they can be plunged outdoors but must be regularly fed and watered if they are to be used again. Re-pot every other year.

RUBBER PLANT see FICUS

RUELLIA (*Acanthaceae*)
MWT 13°C (55°F). Exceptionally attractive South American plants for winter flowering in warm conditions. *R. macrantha* is a bush with large rosy-purple bell flowers in winter, so it rests somewhat in summer but must never dry out. *R. makoyana* is a very attractive trailing plant with dark green prettily marked leaves and rose-red tubular flowers in winter. They need good light without direct sunshine. A half and half mixture of soil-based and peat-based compost suits them. *R. macrantha* (Christmas pride) flowers when small and can be increased by cuttings. *R. makoyana* is also suitable for a hanging basket.

RUSSELIA (*Scrophulariaceae*)
MWT 13°C (55°F). A desirable plant not generally available in Britain but grown in all tropical areas for its long flowering season. It looks rather like an asparagus fern with coral red flowers and is increased by seed or cuttings. Grow in a mixture of soil and peat-based compost in a moist atmosphere. It can be grown in a basket or a tub and will cascade over the edge. *R. juncea* (coral plant), loose racemes of coral red tubular flowers in summer. *R. x lemoinei*, scarlet, is said to flower in winter, both up to 60cm (2ft).

SAINTPAULIA (*Gesneriaceae*)
MWT 16°C (60°F). African violets are not particularly suitable for conservatories but those who dote on them will want them everywhere. They prefer a temperatures between 18°C (65°F) and 24°C (75°F) but a recently introduced hardier strain offers some hope. They came originally from shaded rocky ground in the mountains of Tanzania but those we grow are highly hybridized. Their name *Saintpaulia* is very much simpler than it might have been as they were named after Baron Adalbert Emil Redcliffe Le Tanneur von Saint Paul-Illaire! They need a moist atmosphere, good light and shade from sun. Moisture can be supplied by a pebble tray. Grow in a peat-based compost, allow to dry somewhat between waterings and water minimally if the temperature is low. In ideal conditions they flower all the year round. Increase

by leaf cuttings. There are literally thousands to choose from in various sizes with single or double flowers in many shades, of purple, violet-blue pink and white. Those in a series called 'Ballet' or 'Rhapsodie' are particularly reliable and easy to grow. There are also trailing varieties and miniatures.

SALPIGLOSSIS (*Solanaceae*)
Cold. This tall half hardy annual from Chile has velvety trumpet flowers in beautiful rich colours in summer and autumn. Modern strains are very rewarding if raised from seed in a temperature of 18°C (65°F) in March or April. Grow in soil-based compost using J.I.P.2 for the flowering pot with three plants in a 15 or 18cm (6 or 7in) size. Pinch out growing points when young. F.1 and F.2 hybrids of *S. sinuata*, 45–60cm (18in–2ft).

SALVIA (*Labiatae*)
MWT 10°C (50°F). The sages from Mexico and South America provide a possible source of autumn flowers, particularly in a spacious conservatory with ground beds. *S. involucrata* 'Bethellii' (*Plate 60*) is an autumn-flowering perennial. The shrubby *S. grahamii* is a more pleasing shade of red than the ineffable *S. splendens* used in bedding. *S. neurepia* is more carmine. *S. rutilans*, the pineapple-scented sage, has deep pink flowers in autumn and winter. One can raise the gentian blue *S. patens* from seed in spring and grow it in pots for summer flowering. Grow in soil-based compost. Shrubby salvias are easily rooted from cuttings of flowerless shoots in autumn or spring. Flowering can be delayed by pinching back.

SANSEVIERIA (*Agavaceae*)
MWT 10°C (50°F). 'Mother-in-law's tongue' is a popular foliage plant that some people find hideous. It comes from tropical West Africa and is very easy-going where there is sufficient warmth. Grow in J.I.P.2 with additional sharp sand and do not re-pot until essential. Water minimally in winter, normally in summer and shade from summer sun. Increase by removing rooted offsets. *S. cylindrica* has stiff rolled leaves up to 60cm (2ft); *S. trifasciata* 'Laurentii' with dark green sword-like leaves margined with yellow is the most popular, 45cm (18in). It has an attractive variety in the form of a dwarf rosette of wide stiff leaves with yellow edges, *S. t.* 'Golden Hahnii'.

SASA see BAMBOO

SAXIFRAGA (*Saxifragaceae*)
MWT 10°C (50°F). The nearly hardy *S. stolonifera* from China is an easy foliage plant in shade and poor soil. It is known as 'mother of thousands' and its more brightly coloured and ornamental variety needs this temperature to thrive. It can be grown in a hanging basket with its plantlets hanging round it, or as ground cover. Use any compost and root new runners each year. Water sparingly in winter. *S. stolonifera* (syn. *S. sarmentosa*) 'Tricolor', with dark

green leaves heavily marked with white and pink, has flat rosettes about 15cm (6in) across.

SCARBOROUGH LILY see VALLOTA

SCHIZANTHUS (*Solanaceae*)
MWT 4°C (40°F). Half-hardy annuals from Chile that flower for many weeks with showy orchid-like flowers. The modern hybrids (*Plate 61*) are ever more compact and floriferous but where there is room the tall old-fashioned types may be more graceful. If sown in August they will flower from March to May but must be looked after through the winter. From spring sowings they will flower from June onwards according to temperature and timing. Grow in soil-based compost and pot singly at an early stage. They must be kept growing and will probably need supporting. Grow in good light. Pinching produces a bushy plant with the tall types but is not essential. Hybrids of *S. pinnatus* from dwarfs such as 'Hit Parade', 30cm (1ft), to 'Magnum hybrids', 60–90cm (2–3ft).

SCHLUMBERGERA (*Cactaceae*)
MWT 10°C (50°F). Epiphytic cacti originally from the tropical forests of Brazil and collectively known as Christmas cacti. They have flat drooping branches with showy flowers at their tips. For culture see CACTI. Special points are that they need shade and to be kept moderately moist. They can be outside in summer but must come in by the end of September. They may drop their buds if moved about and subjected to changes of temperature while the buds are forming. Christmas cacti flower at various times from November to March, depending on temperature and treatment. Keep rather dry for a few weeks after flowering. Increase by taking cuttings two joints long and insert two or three together in a small pot of porous compost. Treat as one plant. *S.* x 'Buckleyi' (syn. *S.* 'Bridgesii') is the Christmas cactus with brilliant carmine fuchsia-like flowers around Christmas. *S. truncatus* (syn. *Zygocactus truncatus*) has more claw-like ends to the stems and usually flowers before Christmas. There are many hybrids in various shades of red, coral, pink and white.

SCILLA (*Liliaceae*)
Cold. Hardy dwarf bulbous plants with brilliant blue flowers in early spring. Pot from August to November 2.5cm (1in) deep and close together in J.I.P.2 or other compost. Leave outdoors in a cool place for at least eight weeks before bringing into the conservatory. After flowering, plant out in the garden. *S. bifolia*, turquoise blue, February, 15cm (6in); *S. sibirica* 'Spring Beauty', deep blue, March, 18cm (7in).

SCINDAPSUS (*Araceae*)
MWT 10°C (50°F). An evergreen climbing house plant from tropical Asia closely

related to the philodendrons. Small heart-shaped evergreen leaves are prettily marked with yellow or white in the varieties recommended. They can also be allowed to trail. Grow in soil-based compost, re-potting yearly in spring. Keep only just moist in winter but otherwise water normally and feed occasionally when growing actively. Cut back in spring if necessary. Increase by tip cuttings in spring. *S. aureus* (now correctly called *Epipremnum aureum*), bright green leaves with yellow markings, and particularly *S. a.* 'Marble Queen' with white markings.

SEDUM (*Crassulaceae*)
MWT 4°C (40°F). Some Mexican and Japanese relatives of the hardy stone-crops provide small succulent plants that are easy and decorative when grouped in bowls with other succulents. These are plants for full sun. Grow in soil-based compost with the addition of one third in bulk of coarse sand or perlite. Water moderately in spring and summer and sparingly in winter. *S. lineare* 'Variegatum' is a green and white prostrate creeper to hang over the edge of the staging, yellow flowers; *S. morganianum* (donkey's tail) is a remarkable plant with ropes of pale glaucous green leaves which can hang down 90cm (3ft) in time. It needs some shade and 10°C (50°F). *S. sieboldii* has trailing stems which reach 23cm (9in) and have bunches of pink flowers in October, and *S. s.* 'Medio-Variegatum' with cream blotches in the centres of the leaves which also go pink in sunlight.

SELAGINELLA (*Selaginellaceae*)
MWT 10°C (50°F). A vast family of mossy plants, mostly from tropical America and known as club mosses. They thrive in terrariums or glass containers in moist shade and can also be grown under artificial light. Grow in peat-based compost with some extra sand and keep constantly moist. Increase by layering or take cuttings in summer and grow three as one plant. *S. kraussiana* from South Africa, together with its yellow and variegated forms, is the hardiest. They come in both creeping and upright types and can be used as ground cover in warm shade.

SENECIO (*Compositae*)
Several very different plants in this huge family may be worth growing in the conservatory. There are succulent plants, bedding plants and climbers as well as the familiar *S. cruentus* (which see under CINERARIA). Those mentioned here all come from Africa. *S. articulata* (candle plant) is a succulent with stems like strings of blue-green chippolatas which sprout small leaves in autumn. It is a curiosity of easy culture and different people grow it in different ways. *S. macroglossus* and *S. mikanioides* are both reminiscent of ivy but for growing in sunshine and warmth, while *S. rowleyanus* is a miniature trailing succulent. It looks like strings of peas. Just to confuse things utterly, the familiar silver-leaved plant used for bedding and correctly called *Senecio maritima* is better known as *Cineraria maritima* (which see).

SETCREASEA (*Commelinaceae*)
MWT 7°C (45°F). Easy-going purple-leaved relative of the tradescantias that can be grown in sunlight. Young plants are the most attractive. Grow in soil-based compost and water moderately at all times. They can be grown singly in small pots but are best grouped together in a basket or three to a 15cm (6in) pot. Increase by cuttings in spring or summer. There are small magenta flowers in summer and after flowering some stems will need to be snipped off if they do not continue to grow beyond the flowering point. *S. purpurea* (syn. *S. pallida*, purple heart), a stiff trailer.

SHRIMP PLANT see BELOPERONE

SILVER TREE see LEUCADENDRON

SINNINGIA (*Gesneriaceae*)
MWT 13°C (55°F). This is the botanically correct name for a number of plants generally known under other names. *S. cardinalis* was *Gesneria cardinalis* and then became *Rechsteineria* (which see). Now we have to brace ourselves to call it *Sinningia cardinalis* in the future. The other rechsteineria in this book is correctly *S. leucotricha*. The familiar gloxinias (which see) are really hybrid forms of *S. speciosa*. All these plants need very similar treatment and belong to an increasingly popular family for growing indoors. Some originate in Africa and some in South America but all flourish in warmth and some shade. *Streptocarpus* (which see) is another member of this group. In addition to all these there are smaller and less well known sinningias which are a mixture of small species and offered as seed. They produce charming little rosette plants capable of growing and flowering all the year round (like saintpaulias to which they are also related) and they have variously coloured tubular flowers.

SLIPPER FLOWER see CALCEOLARIA

SLIPPER ORCHID see PAPHIOPEDILUM

SMILAX see ASPARAGUS

SMITHIANTHA (*Gesneriaceae*)
MWT 10°C (50°F). These handsome rhizomatous plants from South America are most suitable for the autumn decoration of a conservatory if there is a warm greenhouse back-up. They like a damp atmosphere, shade from sunlight, and warmth. However the hybrids with their spikes of bell flowers rising above plush-covered leaves are worth a little effort. Grow in peat-based compost with additional perlite to make it porous. In February or March put one rhizome in a 13cm (5in) half pot as they have shallow spreading roots. Water sparingly until they are clearly growing, and freely when they are growing strongly. When they start to die down in October or November, stop watering and rest in their pots until re-potting in spring. Do not store below 10°C (50°F)

and start into growth again in 20°C (70°F) if possible. Hybrids in shades of orange, yellow and pink; S. 'Golden King' with red spotted gold flowers is readily available, 38–60cm (15in–2ft).

SOLANUM (*Solanaceae*)
MWT 10°C (50°F). The little trees with orange-red berries sold around Christmas are either S. *capsicastrum* (winter cherry) from Brazil or S. *pseudocapsicum* (Jerusalem cherry) which is slightly tougher and easier to grow. In a temperature between 10°C (50°F) and 15°C (60°F) it is decorative for a long time. Keep steadily moist but not sodden. Please believe me when I say that this plant is not worth keeping for another year! S. *wendlandii* is a tropical climber with purple potato flowers which can grow in a big pot when young but should be planted out.

SOLLYA (*Pittosporaceae*)
MWT 4°C (40°F). Small Australian evergreen twining climber with clusters of pale blue flowers in early summer. This needs lime-free soil and sun and is best grown in the ground. It can be grown from seed or increased by cuttings of young shoots taken with a heel in spring. S. *heterophylla* (syn. S. *fusiformis*) and S. *parviflora* (syn. S. *drummondii*), both blue, 90cm–1.8m (3–6ft).

SPARMANNIA (*Tiliaceae*)
MWT 7°C (45°F). Quick-growing semi-woody evergreen flowering shrub from Africa. It is sometimes called the indoor lime and has similarly shaped but much larger leaves of a bright fresh green. Clusters of white flowers appear at rather unpredictable intervals. It needs shade from sun. Grow in J.I.P.2. Feed regularly and cut back in early spring to control size. It prefers a temperature around 15° (60°F). This plant comes in several forms with single and double flowers and also a dwarf form which is more compact and free-flowering. This is a good thing as the original plant can grow to 3m (10ft) in time. S. *africana* (African hemp), and its double variety and dwarf form.

SPATHIPHYLLUM (*Araceae*)
MWT 13°C (55°F). Elegant small evergreen relatives of the arum lily from South America, with clusters of glossy leaves and flowers like small arum lilies. They have won a place as house plants where shade and a moist atmosphere are provided. Grow in peat-based compost or a half and half mixture of soil and peat-based compost and keep constantly moist. Increase by careful division in spring. The best known species is S. *wallisii*, with a cream flower and growing to 30cm (1ft); S. 'Mauna Loa' is about twice the size. The flowers gradually change to green but last for some time. It is the leaves that are the attraction.

SPIDER PLANT see CHLOROPHYTUM

SPREKELIA (*Amaryllidaceae*)
MWT 7°C (45°F). Slightly tender Mexican bulbs related to *Hippeastrum* and

flowering in summer. It is known as the Jacobean lily and each bulb has only one flower that lasts up to two weeks. It is less impressive than *Hippeastrum* but survives with less heat. Culture as for *Hippeastrum* but just bury the bulb. *S. formosissima*, curiously shaped deep crimson flowers, early summer, 30cm (1ft).

STAGHORN FERN see PLATYCERIUM

STATICE see LIMONIUM

STEPHANOTIS (*Asclepiadaceae*)
MWT 13°C (55°F). A beautiful evergreen twining climber from Madagascar, with very fragrant white waxy flowers in summer. It is much grown commercially as a pot plant as the flowering time can be adjusted by the manipulation of day length. It is easily affected by fluctuating temperatures so it is not an easy plant in a conservatory. Its preferred temperature is 18–20°C (65–70°F) with a moist atmosphere and shade from sunshine. Grow in J.I.P.2 with a little extra sharp sand and feed with a high potash fertiliser every two weeks from May to September to encourage flowering. Water freely when growing actively, but sparingly when the temperature is low. Re-pot in spring or plant out against a shady wall in the conservatory. *S. floribunda*, white, summer, ultimately 6m (20ft) (*Plate 62*).

STRELITZIA (*Musaceae*)
MWT 10°C (50°F). The bird of paradise flower from South Africa is one of the most remarkable flowers in existence. The flowers look like the head of an exotic bird and last for some weeks. It is a challenging plant for a sunny conservatory, needing a large pot or a tub. It has a leaf formation which allows mealy bugs to breed out of reach or sight! It can be raised from seed but takes about seven years to flower. Water freely in summer but minimally when resting in winter. Feed when in active growth. Grow in J.I.P.2 in a well-drained pot. Re-pot in spring until in the largest pot you are going to give them, then top-dress each spring. They can be increased by division but disturbance is liable to stop flowering for some time. They do best in a sunny position. *S. reginae*, orange and purple flowers in late spring when mature, up to 90cm (3ft).

STREPTOCARPUS (*Gesneriaceae*)
MWT 10°C (50°F). Favourite indoor and greenhouse plants of African origin. The hybrid kinds commonly grown have clusters of leaves rather like primroses which led to their common name of Cape primrose. The freely produced flowers are tubular with a wide mouth and grow several to a stem. There are many hybrid strains available as seed. These will flower in the summer if sown in warmth early in the year. New plants are more easily raised from cuttings of a whole or part of a mature leaf. They will rest in winter

below the temperature of 13°C (55°F) but are capable of growing all the year round. They need shade from sun and regular watering. Grow in either soil-based or peat-based compost. I grow them in an equal mixture of both. Feed with a fertiliser high in phosphate but at half strength every other week in summer. S. 'Constant Nymph', with a constant succession of violet blue flowers, is the best known but there are many others including 'Maasens White'; S. 'John Innes' hybrids range from pale pink to deep purple and some are more compact than others; S. 'Wiesmoor' hybrids are another strain. There are ever more compact F.1 hybrids to raise from seed with names like 'Windowsill Magic' and also mixed seed of the wild species of this interesting group.

STREPTOSOLEN (*Solanaceae*)
MWT 7°C (45°F). Evergreen scandent shrub from Colombia, for growing against a wall, with a wealth of orange bell flowers for months in summer (*Plate 63*). This is a valuable plant for the conservatory border although young plants will flower in pots in J.I.P.2. It likes a sandy soil and a sunny position. Prune back after flowering to keep within bounds. Cuttings of young side shoots root in summer. S. *jamesonii*, orange-scarlet, summer 1.8–2.4m (6–8ft).

STROBILANTHES (*Acanthaceae*)
MWT 16°C (60°F). Foliage plant from Burma valued as a house plant when young for its attractively marked purple flushed leaves which look like enamelled metal. It benefits from frequent renewal from stem cuttings in spring in warmth. This is another plant that does well in an equal mixture of soil-based and peat-based compost. Feed every two weeks while growing actively. S. *dyeranus*, pale blue flowers, up to 60cm (2ft).

SUCCULENTS
This is a very general term to describe plants adapted for surviving periods of drought by storing water in their succulent stems or leaves. In practice any plant from dry areas of the world that we grow in pots tends to become called a succulent and the precise details of their type of succulence is immaterial. We merely want to know how to grow them in our very artificial conditions. They have advantages for us in that they are great survivors of temporary neglect. They are also tolerant of dry air and do not die quickly if not given enough water. Many of the succulents included in this book come from the southern hemisphere. Their natural habitats are not always frost-free but none can be guaranteed to survive the kind of alternately wet and frosty winters with very low light levels that we enjoy. All endure aridity at some time of year in nature and many show an ability to reverse their natural summer and winter to suit us.

Fortunately we do not need to give each of these plants a different compost to match its natural habitat as the majority of them will grow quite happily in any standard mixture which provides sufficient nutrition, porosity and free drainage. The experts use all kinds of variants on the same theme and all of us tend to use a little of what we happen to have. Personally I grow all succulents in J.I.P.2 because it is both nutritous and sterilised. To this I add varying amounts of extra grit or sharp sand, from a sprinkling to up to a quarter of the whole. Others swear by peat-based composts and grow excellent plants. One wants a rather high proportion of sand in the peat compost.

The first necessity of succulent plants is good light. In Britain winter light is inadequate in any case and it is fortunate that most of these plants will rest at this time with a minimum of watering. For instructions to suit some particular plants see under individual entries. The succulent plants in this book (apart from the Cactus family which is treated separately) will be found under AEONIUM, AGAVE, ALOE, COTYLEDON, CRASSULA, ECHEVERIA, EUPHORBIA, GRAPTOPETALUM, HAWORTHIA, JATROPHA, KALANCHOE, PACHYPHYTUM, PEDIL-ANTHUS, ROCHEA, SEDUM, SENECIO and TACITUS.

TACITUS (*Crassulaceae*)
MWT 7°C (45°F). This is a small Mexican succulent and one of the most exciting recently discovered plants to be found in garden centres. It has a flat rosette some 7.5cm (3in) across of tightly packed gunmetal green leaves from which rise several short stalks with clusters of cherry red flowers with white stamens in spring and early summer. They are closely related to *Graptopetalum* and *Echeveria* but neater than either. For cultivation see ECHEVERIA. *T. bellus*, red, spring and summer, 5–7.5cm (2–3in).

TETRASTIGMA (*Vitidaceae*)
MWT 16°C (60°F). The chestnut vine from Indo-China is a tropical tendril climber with glossy leaves divided like a chestnut. It is only suitable for a large steadily heated space and grows at alarming speed unless confined to a pot. In varying temperatures it is inclined to drop sections of stem in the manner of a lizard dropping its tail. Grow in J.I.P.2 and re-pot each year until you want to stop it growing larger. Then top-dress in spring. *T. voinieranum* (syn. *Cissus voinieranum*), ultimately enormous.

THUNBERGIA (*Acanthaceae*)
MWT 10°C (50°F). Annual climber from tropical Africa known as black-eyed Susan and often grown in pots. Sow in warmth in March. Pot three together in small pots of J.I.P.1 or other compost and flower in 12.5 or 15cm (5 or 6in) pots of J.I.P.2. Water freely and shade slightly. *T. alata*, in various shades from cream to orange with purple throat, summer and autumn, up to about 1.8m (6ft).

TIBOUCHINA (*Melastomataceae*)
MWT 10°C (50°F). Evergreen flowering shrub from Brazil with attractive hairy leaves and purple flowers for many months. Grow in soil-based compost. It is

better in a border or tub after the first year and can be trained against a wall. It is a vigorous, sprawling shrub and should be pinched to make a bush. Prune in February or March. *T. semidecandra*, royal purple flowers throughout summer and autumn, ultimately large.

TILLANDSIA (*Bromeliaceae*)
A vast family of bromeliads mainly from South America. They range from tiny lichen-like objects from high mountains to large rosette plants from tropical rain forests. In nature most cling to trees or rocks, or even cacti in the drier areas, and have become known as 'air plants' because of their capacity to absorb moisture from the atmosphere through their scaly leaves. Those with grey and scurfy foliage tend to come from misty areas and the green kinds from the forests. For decoration their main use is as the plants with which to make a bromeliad tree, for which they are particularly suitable as many can be maintained quite healthily by regular spraying with rain water when fixed to a branch with a little sphagnum moss round their rudimentary roots. For a wide choice one has to go to a specialist nursery but a number are on sale at garden centres. The most frequently seen is the spectacular *T. cyanea* with brilliant blue flowers round a pink head of bracts above a rosette of shiny green leaves up to 30cm (1ft) across. This is not an easy plant and needs MWT 13°C (55°F) to thrive. There are vast numbers of smaller grey plants such as *T. argentea* with pink flowers and the various forms of *T. ionantha* (with purple flowers when mature) which are easy to please and look much more lively when established than when bought dry and cold. These are mostly quite satisfied with MWT 10°C (50°F). See also BROMELIADS.

TOLMIEA (*Saxifragaceae*)
MWT 4°C (40°F). A hardy herbaceous plant with hairy heart-shaped leaves that is grown as a foliage plant in shade. It has the great attraction that new plantlets develop on its leaves, from which it is easily increased. Known as pig-a-back plant, this is one of those that is passed from hand to hand. They can be planted three together in a pot and grown in soil-based compost. They can also be grouped in a hanging basket. *T. menziesii* and also its variegated variety, with yellow speckling.

TORENIA (*Scrophulariaceae*)
Cold. Half-hardy annual from Vietnam which is one of the most attractive annuals to grow in pots for summer flowering. This is a plant that appreciates warmth and a moist atmosphere although it can be flowered in summer without heat. Sow in March or April in a temperature of 16°C (60°F). Pot singly and pinch several times to make bushy. Shade from hot summer sun. Give twiggy support and flower in 12.5 or 15cm (5 or 6in) pots of J.I.P.2. *T. fournieri*, lavender-blue with yellow throat and purple tips, 30cm (1ft).

TRACHELIUM (*Campanulaceae*)

MWT 7°C (45°F). Sub-shrubby perennial from southern Europe, grown for its dense heads of tiny blue flowers. It can be grown as a half-hardy annual to flower in 12.5cm (5in) pots but better plants are produced by growing it as a biennial. Pot firmly in J.I.P.2 and pinch several times to make a shapely plant with a number of flowering heads. A good plant takes space and a big pot. A poor plant is easy but not worth growing. It can be sown from February to June and will flower when you allow its tall flowering stems to develop. Feed when the pots are full of roots. Water freely. *T. caeruleum*, mauvy-blue, 45–90cm (18in–3 ft).

TRACHELOSPERMUM (*Apocynaceae*)
Cold. Slightly tender evergreen twining climber from China with fragrant white flowers. It is sometimes called Chinese jasmine. Young plants can be grown in pots in the same manner as *Jasminum polyanthum*. Otherwise it is better in a border. Water freely in summer. Prune back immediately after flowering. *T. jasminioides* (syn. *Rhynchospermum jasminoides*), white, summer, 4.5m (15ft).

TRACHYCARPUS see PALMS

TRADESCANTIA (*Commelinaceae*)
MWT 13°C (55°F). Easily grown small evergreen trailers from South America, known as wandering Jew. They are usually grown in their variegated forms for their leaves which are striped with white, yellow or purple. Cuttings can be rooted in a glass of water and several are grown together. Grow in soil-based compost and renew frequently from cuttings. Most people do not distinguish between plants called CALLISEA, SETCREASIA and ZEBRINA (which see). They are all grown and used in the same way to hang over the front of staging or trail from hanging baskets. *T. albiflora* 'Albovittata', white striped leaves; *T. a.* 'Aurea', yellow leaves and *T. a.* 'Tricolor', leaves striped with purple and white; *T. fluminensis*, very similar with forms with white or cream stripes; *T. f.* 'Quicksilver', a strong white striped one with larger leaves and more white flowers.

TRANSVAAL DAISY see GERBERA

TRICHOSPORUM see AESCHYNANTHUS

TROPAEOLUM (*Tropaeolaceae*)
MWT 10°C (50°F). A tuberous-rooted climber from Chile with pretty, five-lobed leaves and scarlet, yellow and maroon flowers in spring. Pot the dormant tubers singly in summer in soil-based compost and water very sparingly until growth shows. Water carefully always as it is easy to rot the tuber. Give twiggy support. Dry off completely when the leaves turn yellow and re-pot each year. Increase by seed sown when ripe. *P. tricolorum*, scarlet flowers with yellow centres and maroon markings, spring, 90cm (3ft).

TULIPA (*Liliaceae*)
Cold. Hardy bulbs for early flowers. With glass protection everything flowers earlier and some of the smaller earlier tulips can be welcome in a conservatory. The choice must be a personal one but I would suggest *T. praestans* 'Fusilier' and the early single and double tulips with the shortest stems. Pot up in October or November in soil-based compost and plunge outdoors or keep in a cellar or unheated conservatory. They must come into the light when the shoots are about 2.5cm (1in) long. Do not allow them to dry out before flowering.

UMBRELLA PLANT see CYPERUS

VALLOTA (*Amaryllidaceae*)
MWT 7°C (45°F). Evergreen African bulbous plant with scarlet trumpet flowers in late summer. It is related to *Hippeastrum* and sometimes called the Scarborough lily. It is decorative only when in flower for about two weeks but then it is a triumph. It is best acquired in a pot and not as a dry bulb. Pot firmly in J.I.P.2. Water sparingly until growing well and only keep just moist in winter but water freely in summer. Grow in full sun. Re-pot only every three or four years as they flower best when pot-bound. Feed in summer when established and give tomato fertiliser in late summer. Increase by dividing the clump of bulbs that develops. Small side bulbs take several years to flower which they do when about the size of a tulip bulb. A flowering-size bulb should have a 12.5cm (5in) pot. *V. speciosa* (syn. *V. purpurea*), bright scarlet, late summer, about 38cm (15in). There are said to be white, and salmon-coloured variants.

VELTHEIMIA (*Liliaceae*)
MWT 4°C (40°F). Bulbous plant from southern Africa with handsome glossy foliage in winter and flowers like small red-hot-pokers in early spring. Pot in August or September singly in 12.5cm (5in) pots in J.I.P.2 or similar compost, leaving the nose of the bulb exposed. Water moderately when growing and feed when flower buds are developing. Dry off gradually after flowering and keep quite dry in their pots until August. Re-pot at least every other year. There is some confusion about the naming of these plants but those on sale are easy and worth growing in cool conditions. I have only come across two species, *V. capensis* with wavy leaves and its variety 'Rosalba' with pink and cream flowers, and *V. viridifolia*, with wider straighter leaves and flowers of a deeper pink. They both reach about 38cm (15in) when in full flower.

VITIS (*Vitidaceae*)
Cold. A grape vine under glass which faces south can produce delicious fruit, wine and welcome shade but the successful growing of grapes is quite complicated and does not combine at all well with other activities. A healthy

vine needs to be cold in winter and very freely ventilated in both winter and summer. It also gives too much shade in summer for many plants to grow underneath it. The roots are greedy and are best confined. However, grown purely for sitting under, it can be planted in a tub and trained to go where you want it. The time to cut it hard back is when the leaves have fallen.

VRIESIA (*Bromeliaceae*)
MWT 16°C (60°F). Impressive bromeliads from South America with large rosettes of stiff leaves which are attractively marked. *V. splendens* is well known with its spear of scarlet bracts and striped foliage. For the connoisseur *V. fenestralis* and *V. hieroglyphica* are two very choice, rare and expensive plants with beautiful netted patterns on their leaves. They can be admired at shows but are rarely for sale. For culture see BROMELIADS.

WANDERING JEW see TRADESCANTIA

WASHINGTONIA (*Palmae*)
MWT 4°C (40°F). Fan palms from Southern California and Mexico which are reasonably adaptable for growing in pots and tubs when young. These palms need to be watered very freely in summer and kept almost dry in winter. Re-pot only when roots appear on the surface of the soil. For culture see PALMS. *W. filifera* is the petticoat palm; *W. robusta* is faster growing with stiffer foliage.

WAX FLOWER see HOYA

WINTER CHERRY see SOLANUM
YUCCA (*Agavaceae*)
MWT 10°C (50°F). Spiky, palm-like plants with one or more rosettes of leaves at the top of a tall stem. The one on sale in every supermarket is *Y. elephantipes* from Guatemala. This has softer leaves than the others and no spines. A rather hardier kind is *Y. aloifolia*, known as Spanish bayonet, which has very sharply-pointed leaves. There are variegated-leaved kinds of both. Grow in soil-based compost and preferably in clay or ceramic pots as they easily become top-heavy. They appreciate strong light. Water freely in summer and sparingly in winter. Feed when growing actively and re-pot in spring when necessary. *Y. aloifolia*, green leaves; *Y. a. draconis*, soft leaves on a branching plant; *Y. a. marginata*, with yellow-edged leaves; *Y. a. quadricolor* has reddish and white as well as yellow stripes; *Y. a. tricolor* has central white and yellow central stripes; and *Y.a.*'Variegata' with white stripes. They can grow to 90cm–1.2m (3–4ft) ultimately in pots.

ZANTEDESCHIA (*Araceae*)
MWT 13°C (55°F). Rhizomatous plants from Southern Africa, known as arum lilies. Although some are hardy in some parts of the country they have long been persuaded to flower in winter and early spring under glass, as their fleshy

roots can be wakened from a dry resting period at a time to suit the grower. The well known Z. *aethiopica*, the white arum lily, is a large fleshy plant and it is more interesting to grow the more compact varieties listed below. The yellow Z. *elliottiana* is more tender and is potted in February to flower in summer. Z. *rehmanii* is a smaller plant with narrower leaves and smaller flowers of pink to purple. There are also hybrids between these plants which may be offered. Use a soil-based compost, putting a single plant in a 15cm (6in) pot or grouped together in larger containers. Cover the rhizomes with 5cm (2in) of soil and water sparingly at first but freely when they are in full leaf. These are marsh plants and among the few that can stand in a saucer of water. They will need feeding regularly until the flowers are over. After flowering reduce watering and dry off completely when the leaves yellow. Keep dry in their pots until starting into growth once more. Z. *aethiopica*, white spathes with yellow central spadix in winter or early spring from early autumn planting, up to 90cm (3ft); Z. *a.* 'Childsiana' is smaller and more free-flowering; Z. *elliottiana*, golden yellow, summer, spotted leaves, 60cm (2ft); Z. *rehmannii*, pink, summer, about 38cm (15in).

ZEBRINA (*Commelinaceae*)
MWT 13°C (55°F). Trailing evergreen foliage plant from Mexico with prettily striped leaves. They grow fast and need pinching to make them branch. For culture see TRADESCANTIA to which these are closely related, but a little more tender. Z. *pendula*, green leaves with irridescent silvery stripes, together with its varieties with even more colourful stripes and purple backs to the leaves. The most attractive one known as Z. *pendula* 'Quadricolor', with pink, cream and silver stripes, is also the most difficult to grow.

ZYGOCACTUS see SCHLUMBERGERA

Glossary

AERIAL ROOTS. Roots that absorb moisture direct from the air and often secure plants to trees or rocks in nature.

ANNUAL. A plant grown from seed to flower in a single season only.

BIENNIAL. A plant that reaches the flowering stage only in its second season and then dies.

BRACT. A modified leaf that is sometimes brightly coloured and mistaken for a flower (as in *Bougainvillea* and poinsettia).

BROMELIAD. A plant belonging to the family *Bromeliaceae*.

BULB. The storage organ of a plant with a dormant period. It is usually underground and contains embryo leaves and even flowers. See also corm, rhizome and tuber.

CAUDEX. A swollen base to the stem of some plants from dry regions.

CORM. Underground storage organ which sometimes has a tunic (as in crocus).

CULTIVAR. A variety of a plant whose characteristics are preserved by some means of controlled propagation.

CUTTING. A piece of a plant (usually the stem) which can be made to grow roots and form a new plant. Roots and leaves of certain plants can also be used.

DECIDUOUS. Plants that lose their leaves at the end of each growing season and renew them annually.

EPIPHYTE. A plant that uses aerial roots to support itself and may cling to trees and rocks but is not a parasite.

ERICACEOUS. A member of the heather family (*Ericaceae*) and usually lime-hating.

FAMILY. In the classification of living organisms the group larger than a genus which in turn is larger than a species. For example *Abutilon megapotamicum* is a species (*megapotamicum*) of the genus *Abutilon* which is a member of the family *Malvaceae*.

GENUS. A number of related species which botanists have collected under a single name. See FAMILY.

HABITAT. The native home in the wild of a plant.

HERBACEOUS. Plants that do not form a woody stem.

HYBRID. A plant produced by crossing two different plants within a genus. Occasionally this is done between different but closely related genera.

OFFSET. A new plant that develops naturally at the base of a mature plant and can be used for propagation. Bulbs, bromeliads and cacti often produce offsets. An offshoot is similar.

PALMATE. A leaf shaped roughly like a hand.

PERENNIAL. A plant that lives for at least three seasons and usually indefinitely.

PINCHING-OUT. Removing the growing tip of a plant to encourage bushyness.

PINNATE. Leaves with a row of smaller leaflets (pinnae) on either side of the stalk. Bi-pinnate means a further division, as in many ferns.

PRICKING-OUT. Re-planting seedlings spaced out with room to grow in fresh soil.

PROPAGATION. The creation of new plants by any means including seed sowing.

PSEUDO BULB. The thickened bulb-like stem of an orchid used for water storage.

RACEME. A cluster of flowers on individual but unbranched stalks as in a hyacinth.

RHIZOME. A fleshy underground stem that usually spreads horizontally and produces new shoots away from the parent.

SPATHE. A large bract enclosing flowers which sometimes resembles a flower (as in *Anthurium* and *Arum*).

SPECIES. See FAMILY.

SPORE. The dust-like single cells by which ferns and mosses start their reproductive processes.

SUCCULENT. A plant with fleshy stems or leaves that can store moisture in dry regions or conditions.

TERRARIUM. A sealed container made of glass or plastic in which plants are grown.

TERRESTRIAL. Growing in the ground.

TOP-DRESS. To add fresh soil or fertiliser to plants without disturbing the roots. In pots it means carefully removing a little of the surface soil and replacing it with new and enriched compost.

TUBER. A fleshy root like a potato, used for food storage during a resting season.

TUBERCLE. Nodules or swellings on a plant body, notably of cacti.

VARIETY. Strictly speaking this is a naturally occurring variation of a wild species. But it is loosely, and generally, used to refer to any variations in cultivated plants (see CULTIVAR).

Useful Addresses

Alexander Bartholomew Conservatories Ltd
Kilmuir, North Kessock, Inverness and 83 Disraeli Road, London SW15 2DY.
Quality modular designs. Timber conservatories with single or double glazing, also solar-control or safety glass.

Alite Metals Ltd
9 Maze Street, Barton Hill, Bristol, BS5 9TE
Aluminium sections only for the DIY enthusiast.

Alitex Ltd
Station Road, Alton, Hampshire GU35 2PZ
Aluminium glasshouses and conservatories

Amdega Ltd
Faverdale Industrial Estate, Darlington, Co. Durham DL3 0PW and Zodiac House, 163 London Road, Croydon, Surrey CR0 0XL
Superior timber conservatories, including custom-built and double-glazed.

Baco Leisure Products Ltd
Windover Road, Huntingdon, Cambridgeshire PE18 7EH
Metal conservatories at popular prices.

Banbury Homes and Gardens Ltd
PO Box 17, Banbury, Oxfordshire OX17 3NS
Standard modular designs in metal with various finishes, single- or double-glazed.

Clear Span Ltd
Wellington Road, Greenfield, Nr Oldham, Lancashire OL3 7AG
Solid aluminium alloy conservatories.

Crittal Warmlife Ltd
Crittal Road, Witham, Essex CMB8 3AW
Metal conservatories.

Crusader Conservatories Ltd
Neville Road, North Tees Industrial Estate, Stockton-on-Tees, Cleveland TS18 2RD
Wide range of traditional cedar conservatories.

Edenlite Products
Wern Works, Briton Ferry, Neath, Glamorgan SA11 2JS
Standard aluminium alloy designs.

Florada Garden Products
Dollar Street House, Cirencester, Gloucestershire GL7 2AP
Metal conservatories with bronze finish and curved design.

Gardens Under Glass
Prospect House, 133 White Lion Road Amersham, Buckinghamshire HP6 6BE
Conservatory interior design, advice and plant selection by post.

Halls Homes and Gardens Ltd
Church Road, Paddock Wood, Tonbridge, Kent TN12 6EU
Aluminium lean-to conservatories, painted or natural.

Machin Designs Ltd
4 Avenue Studios, Sydney Close, London SW3 6HW
Workshops at Stafford. Elegant designs in wood and metal with white finish for conservatories and pool-houses.

Marley Buildings Ltd
Peasmarsh, Guildford, Surrey GU3 1LS
Standard metal lean-to conservatories

Marston and Langinger Ltd
Hall Staithe, Fakenham, Norfolk NR21 9BW

Robinsons of Winchester Ltd
Robinson House, Winnall Industrial
Estate, Winchester, Hampshire SO23
8LH
Metal-framed conservatories with sliding
doors and twin-wall polycarbonate roofs.

Room Outside Ltd
Goodwood Gardens, Waterbeach,
Nr Chichester, Sussex PO18 oQB
Architect designed adaptable modular
timber conservatories with aluminium
glazing-bars in roofs.

Turner Conservatories Ltd
Fumbally works, Blackpitts, Dublin 8,
Ireland and 293/295 Bath Road,
Hounslow West, Middlesex TW3 3DB
Aluminium lean-to conservatories of
curvilinear design.

Rosedale Engineers Ltd
Rosedale Works, Hunmany, Filey,
Yorkshire.
Solardomes – metal-framed domed
glasshouses with a circular base.

Wessex Aluminium Ltd
Dunbeath Road, Elgin Industrial Estate,
Swindon, Wiltshire SN2 6EA.
Metal lean-to conservatories – curved or
conventional design.

Whitehouse, C.H.Ltd
Buckhurst Works, Frant, Tunbridge
Wells, Kent TN3 9BN
Cedarwood conservatories made to
order.

York Conservatories
Hull Road, Kexby, York YO4 5LE

Sources of seeds, plants and compost

Seeds

Thomas Butcher Ltd
60 Wickham Road
Shirley
Croydon, Surrey

Chiltern Seeds
Bortree Stile
Ulverston, Cumbria LA2 7PB

Dickson Brown & Tait Ltd
Attenbury's Lane, Timperly,
Altrincham, Cheshire WA14 5QL

Samuel Dobie & Sons Ltd
Upper Dee Mills, Llangollen
Clwyd LL20 4BE

C.W.Hosking Exotic Seed Importer
PO Box 500, Hayle
Cornwall TR27 4BE

Suttons Seeds
Hele Road, Torquay
Devon TQ2 7QT

Thompson & Morgan
London Road, Ipswich
Suffolk IP2 0BA

Plants

Anmore Exotics
4 The Curve, Lovedean
Hampshire PO8 9SE
(Unusual tropical plants and indoor
design).

Monica Bennet
Cypress Nursery, Powke Lane
Blackheath, Birmingham
(Pelargoniums, fuchsias and conservatory
plants).

C.G.Clarke
Westdale Gardens, Holt Road
Bradford-on-Avon, Wiltshire
(Pelargoniums, fuchsias and conservatory
plants).

Findlay Clark Ltd
Boclair Road, Milngavie
Glasgow G62 6EP
(Tropical and other plants).

Clifton Nurseries
Clifton Villas, Warwick Avenue
London W9
(Wide choice of plants and containers).

Long Man Gardens
Lewes Road, Wilmington
Polegate, East Sussex BN26 5RS

Newington Nurseries
Newington, Nr Oxford

Read's Nurseries
Loddon, Norfolk
(Citrus, grapes and figs).

B.Wall (Mail order only)
4 Selbourne Close, New Haw
Weybridge, Surrey
(Mainly begonias and bromeliads).

Westfield Plants
Great Chalfield, Melksham
Wiltshire
(Unusual frost-free conservatory plants).

Woodhouse Plants
Lower End, Swaffham Prior
Cambridge CB5 0HT

Specialist Nurseries

ACHIMENES

K.J.Townsend
17 Valerie Close, St Albans
Hertfordshire AL1 5JD

BEGONIAS

Blackmore & Langdon
Stanton Nurseries, Pensford
Nr Bristol

BROMELIADS

Vesutor Ltd
The Bromeliad Nursery
Billinghurst Lane, Ashington
West Sussex RH20 3BA

CACTI

Abbey Brook Cactus Nursery
Old Hackney Lane, Matlock
Derbyshire

Cruck Cottage Cacti
Wrelton, Pickering
North Yorkshire

Holly Gate Cactus Nursery
Ashington
West Sussex RH20 3BA

Westfield Cacti
10 Shillingford Road
Exeter EX2 8UB

Whitestone Gardens Ltd
The Cactus Houses
Sutton-under-Whitestonecliffe
Thirsk, North Yorkshire YO7 2PZ

FERNS

J.K.Marston
Culag, Green Lane
Nafferton, Nr Driffield
East Yorkshire

FUCHSIAS

Fuchsialand
77/83 Chester Road
New Oscott
Lancashire B73 5BA

Hills Fuchsias
Hunwick Station
Nr Crook
County Durham DL15 0RB

C.S.Lockyer
70 Henfield Road
Coalpit Heath
Bristol BS17 2UZ

Kathleen Muncaster Fuchsias
18 Field Lane
Gainsborough
Lincolnshire DN21 3BY

Mayes Fuchsias
Mayes Lane
Sandon
Essex

NERINES

Nerine Nurseries
Welland
Worcestershire WR13 6LN

ORCHIDS

Devon Orchid Centre
Forges Cross
Newton abbot
Devon

Mansell & Hatcher Ltd
Cragg Wood Nurseries
Rawdon, Leeds LS19 6LQ

McBeans Orchids Ltd
Cooksbridge, Lewes
Sussex BN8 4PR

Randalls Orchids
Highland Hall
Monks Eleigh
Nr Ipswich
Suffolk

Ratcliffe Orchids Ltd
Chilton, Didcot
Oxfordshire OX11 0RT

Wyld Court Orchids
Hampstead Norreys
Newbury
Berkshire RG16 0TN

PALMS

The Palm Centre
22 Guildford Road
London SW8 2BX The Palm Farm
Thornton Hall Gardens
Ulceby
South Humberside DB39 6XF

PELARGONIUMS

Beckwood Nurseries
New Inn Road, Beckly
Nr Oxford Clapton Court Gardens
Nr Crewkerne Somerset
(also fuchsias).

Fibrex Nurseries Ltd
Harvey Road, Evesham
Worcestershire
(also ferns and ivies).

The Vernon Geranium Nursery
Hill End Road, Harefield
Uxbridge, Middlesex UB9 6LH
(cuttings by mail order).

STREPTOCARPUS

Efenechtyd Nurseries
Llanedlidan, Ruthin
Clwyd

WATER LILIES

Bennett's Water Lily and Fish Farm
Chickerell, Weymouth
Dorset DT3 4AF

Compost

HDRA Sales Ltd
National Centre for Organic Gardening
Ruyton-on-Dunsmore, Coventry CV8
3LG
Organic composts, safe pesticides and
biological controls

John Innes Manufacturers' Association
19 High Street, Theale, Berkshire RG7
5AH
Information about John Innes Composts

Orchid Sundries
99a Kiln Ride
Wokingham, Berkshire RG11 3PD
Mail order composts, etc.

Silvapearl Products Ltd
PO Box 8, Harrogate,
North Yorkshire HG2 8JW
Perlite, vermiculite and composts

Index

Note: For the sake of concision only generic names of plants are indexed. Within the *Dictionary of Plants* the full specific names are given.